OSPREY MILITARY CAMPAIGN SERIES: 54

SHILOH 1862

THE DEATH OF INNOCENCE

D1428099

SERIES EDITOR: LEE JOHNSON

OSPREY MILITARY CAMPAIGN SERIES: 54

SHILOH 1862

THE DEATH OF INNOCENCE

TEXT BY
JAMES R. ARNOLD

BATTLESCENE PLATES BY
ALAN & MICHAEL PERRY

OSPREY
MILITARY

First published in Great Britain in 1998 by Osprey Publishing,
Elms Court, Chapel Way, Botley, Oxford OX2 9LP United Kingdom

ISBN 1 85532 606 X

Editor: Iain MacGregor
Design: The Black Spot

Colour bird's eye view illustrations by Peter Harper
Cartography by Micromap
Wargaming Shiloh 1862 by Jim Webster
Battlescene artwork by Alan and Michael Perry
Filmset in Singapore by Pica Ltd.
Printed through World Print Ltd., Hong Kong

98 99 00 01 02   10 9 8 7 6 5 4 3 2 1

FOR A CATALOGUE OF ALL BOOKS PUBLISHED BY OSPREY MILITARY PLEASE WRITE TO:
The Marketing Manager, Osprey Publishing Ltd., P.O. Box 140,
Wellingborough, Northants NN8 4ZA United Kingdom

Key to military series symbols

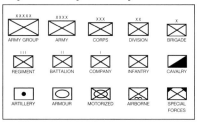

Acknowledgements

I wish to thank the helpful people at Andre Studio/Rockbridge
Camera Shop; Robert C. Arnold for his photographic work at the
Tennessee State Library and Archives; the co-operative staff at the
Library of Congress and National Archives; Shiloh National Military
Park; Washington & Lee University; and my editor nonpareil, Roberta
Wiener.

Publisher's note

Readers may wish to study this title in conjunction with the following
Osprey publications:

MAA 37 *Army of Northern Virginia*
MAA 38 *Army of the Potomac*
MAA 170 *American Civil War Armies (1) Confederate*
MAA 177 *American Civil War Armies (2) Union*
MAA 179 *American Civil War Armies (3) Specialist Troops*
MAA 190 *American Civil War Armies (4) State Troops*
MAA 207 *American Civil War Armies (5) Volunteer Militias*
MAA 252 *Flags of the American Civil War (1) Confederate*
MAA 258 *Flags of the American Civil War (2) Union*
MAA 265 *Flags of the American Civil War (3) State and Volunteer*
WAR 6 *Confederate Infantryman 1861-65*
WAR 13 *Union Cavalryman 1861-65*
Elite 62 *American Civil War Zouaves*
CAM 10 *First Bull Run 1861*
CAM 17 *Chickamauga 1863*
CAM 26 *Vicksburg 1863*
CAM 32 *Antietam 1862*
CAM 52 *Gettysburg 1863*

Artist's note

Readers may care to note the original paintings from which the colour
plates in this book were prepared are available for private sale. All
reproduction copyright whatsoever is retained by the publisher.
Enquiries should be addressed to:
    3 Quorn Close, Attenborough Close, Nottingham NG9 6BU

The publishers regret that they can enter into no correspondence
upon this matter.

PAGE 2 **Young midwestern men flocked to the colours in
1861 out of a sense of patriotism and adventure. In both
North and South, great patriotic displays marked the receipt
of the flag by the volunteers. (Library of Congress)**

TITLE PAGE **Nine-year-old John Clem ran away from home
to join the army in 1861 as a drummer, and a shell smashed
his drum at Shiloh. Later, he exchanged his drum for a cut-
down musket appropriate to his size because 'I did not like
to stand and be shot at without shooting back'. When an
enemy officer rode up and demanded 'Surrender you
damned little Yankee!' at Chickamauga, Clem shot him from
his saddle. He remained in the army after the war eventually
rising to the rank of major-general. (National Archives)**

CONTENTS

ORIGINS OF THE CAMPAIGN

The United States' strategic plan to subjugate the Confederate States of America regarded the Mississippi River as a corridor of invasion which could split the Confederacy. Key to the Mississippi was the border state of Kentucky. When war began, Kentucky maintained an uneasy neutrality as forces massed just over its northern and southern borders. Many believed that whichever side entered Kentucky first would throw the state into the hands of its rival.

Unperturbed by this, in the autumn of 1861 Confederate commander Major-General Leonidas Polk marched his men into Kentucky, believing that his move would pre-empt a Yankee offensive by Brigadier-General U.S. Grant. Polk's impetuosity proved a mistake simply because the Yankees had more resources to bring to bear than did Polk. Grant countered Polk by rapidly occupying Paducah, in southwest Kentucky. Soon afterwards other Federal forces marched over the Ohio River into the Bluegrass State. Suddenly unshielded, the Confederacy lay vulnerable from the Mississippi River east to the mountains.

Confederate President Jefferson Davis dispatched the man he considered the nation's ablest officer, General Albert Sidney Johnston, to the threatened sector. Johnston boldly advanced his small army to Bowling Green, Kentucky, and by so doing frightened his opponents into inactivity. Johnston stretched his forces to the breaking point as he tried to form a defensive arc covering the crucial Tennessee border. It was all a colossal bluff that gave false assurances to Confederate leaders, a bluff that Johnston knew would collapse when the Yankees found an aggressive fighting general.

The 1st Arkansas marched to battle at Shiloh cheering Sidney Johnston. Johnston responded, 'Shoot low boys; it takes two to carry one off the field.' He told its colonel, 'I hope you may get through safely today, but we must win a victory.' (National Archives)

Confederate artillery sited on the Cumberland River stopped the Union gunboats at Fort Donelson. (Author's collection)

In the third week of January 1862, Johnston sent his superiors in Richmond an urgent dispatch: 'All the resources of the Confederacy are now needed for the defence of Tennessee.' It was too late. Two weeks later, just as Johnston feared, the North found the determined officer who was willing to take risks. Grant advanced to capture Forts Henry and Donelson, the twin pillars that guarded western Tennessee, and thereby opened the way to the Confederate heartland.

Across a 150-mile front stretching from the middle of Tennessee to the Mississippi River, three Federal armies lay poised to invade. To the west, Major-General John Pope's 25,000-man force prepared to advance against a series of forts and batteries that blocked Federal naval movement down the Mississippi River. To the east, Major-General Don Carlos Buell massed a 50,000-man force at Nashville. In the centre,

CONVERGENCE ON SHILOH, MARCH 1862

By stripping-in secondary theatres, the Confederacy assembles an army at Corinth under the command of A.S. Johnston. The plan is to defeat Grant before his army unites with Buell.

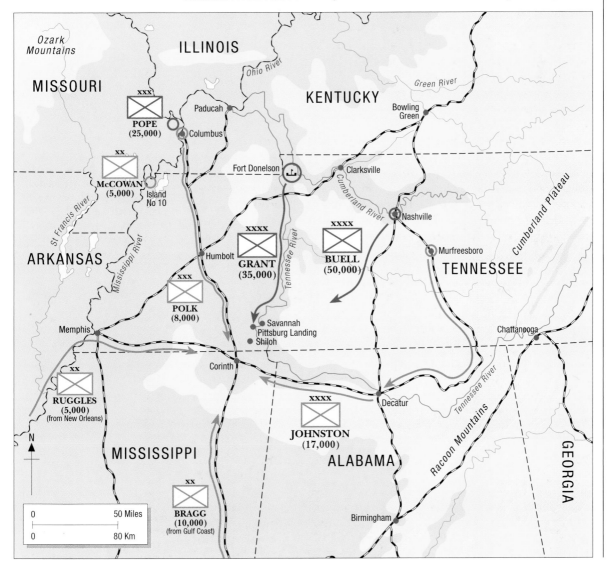

Grant's men moved up the Tennessee River towards the important rail hub at Corinth, Mississippi. If these three armies co-operated, the out-numbered rebels would be hard pressed to oppose them.

At this time of crisis Confederate Maj.Gen. Braxton Bragg was serving in a backwater command comprising Alabama and west Florida. From that vantage point he offered a persuasive strategic analysis. Bragg believed that the Confederate forces were too scattered. He recommended that secondary points be abandoned, that troops be ruthlessly stripped from garrison duty in order to concentrate at the point of decision, the portion of Tennessee occupied by Grant's army. Bragg was certain that 'We have the right men, and the crisis upon us demands they should be in the right places'. General P.G.T. Beauregard also believed in the virtues of concentration and agreed with Bragg. It would require a complex massing of men from five different independent commands. By rail, steamboat, and foot, soldiers would move from places as far distant as Mobile and New Orleans to join Sidney Johnston at Corinth. The planned counteroffensive was a high stakes gamble, but Jefferson Davis approved. The Confederate president understood that success hinged upon two factors: surprise; and striking before Grant received reinforcements from Buell.

Unbeknown to the rebel high command, several factors were working in favour of the counter-offensive. On 4 March 1862, Union Major-General Halleck relieved Grant of command because of alleged neglect and inefficiency. Grant's senior divisional commander, General C.F. Smith, replaced him and began a march south from Fort Donelson in the direction of Corinth. As Smith advanced along the Tennessee River, he called upon a newly raised division under the command of William T. Sherman to raid downstream to cut the Memphis and Charleston Railroad. When this expedition became bogged down in tor-rential rains, Sherman sought a temporary base. He disembarked his men at the first place above water. Located on the western bank of the Tennessee River, its name was Pittsburg Landing. Inland, about four miles to the south, was Shiloh Church. The soaking Federal soldiers did not know that the ground from the landing to this church would become the scene of terrible battle.

Meanwhile, when President Abraham Lincoln heard that Halleck had relieved Grant, he was not happy. Lincoln was not about to lose his best (and at this point in the war apparently his only) fighting general. Down the chain of command came word that Halleck would have to provide detailed, specific information about the basis for his decision to relieve Grant. Although at times Halleck possessed a keen strategic mind, he was most comfortable when engaging in a hectoring, paper war against his subordinates. Like most bullies, when confronted with rival force he backed down. So it was when he received the War Department's request regarding Grant. Correctly judging the political winds, he wrote to Grant, 'Instead of relieving you, I wish you as soon as your new army is in the field to assume the immediate command and lead it on to new victories.'

With characteristic energy, Grant began forwarding troops to the camps around Pittsburg Landing. If the recent battle at Fort Donelson had proved anything, it was that his soldiers badly needed instruction and discipline. The clearings and fields inland from Pittsburg Landing seemed to offer fine ground for a large camp of instruction. As more and more soldiers arrived, their officers distributed them without regard to tactical considerations. Instead, the various divisions occupied sites based upon proximity to water, firewood, and open ground for drill. No-one seriously anticipated the possibility of fighting a battle here. Two days before the rebel onslaught, Sherman informed Grant that 'I do not apprehend anything like an attack on our position.'

In Richmond, the first week of April 1862 was one of near unbearable suspense for the Confederate commander-in-chief. Davis wanted to travel west to participate in the pending battle, but was forced to remain in Richmond because a massive Union army commanded by the woefully misnamed 'Young Napoleon', Maj.Gen. George B. McClellan, was slowly advancing upon the Confederate capital. Still, Davis expected nothing but good news from Tennessee, telling friends that after Sidney Johnston's victory the future would brighten. To Johnston himself he sent an eve of battle telegram saying, 'I anticipate victory.'

So spring came to western Tennessee, with Grant's unsuspecting Union army about to face a major assault from a Confederate force desperately in need of success.

CHRONOLOGY

1860
November – Abraham Lincoln elected President.
December – South Carolina votes to secede from the Union.

1861
9 February – Jefferson Davis elected President of the Confederate States of America.
12 April – P.G.T. Beauregard supervises bombing of Fort Sumter.
30 August – A.S. Johnston named top-ranking Confederate field

general; Beauregard also on list of top five.

September – A.S. Johnston arrives west to assume command of all Confederate forces from Arkansas to Cumberland Gap.

7 November – U.S. Grant conducts the battle of Belmont.

1862

4-16 February – Forts Henry and Donelson campaign.

1-24 March – Confederate concentration at Corinth.

11 March – Halleck assumes command of department including the armies of Pope, Grant and Buell.

15 March – Sherman's Division arrives at Pittsburg Landing.

16 March – Buell begins march to join Grant.

29 March – A.S. Johnston assumes command of Army of the Mississippi in Corinth.

3 April – Army of the Mississippi begins approach march from Corinth.

4 April – 5th Ohio Cavalry encounters Hardee's Corps.

5 April – Balance of Confederate army straggles into position before Shiloh and encounters Union patrols.

6 April

0300 Hrs – Powell begins reconnaissance.

0500 Hrs – Combat in Fraley Field.

0630 Hrs – Confederate line advances.

0700 Hrs – Sherman under fire.

0800 Hrs – McClernand and Hurlbut begin to support front line.

0830 Hrs – Grant arrives at Landing.

0900 Hrs – Prentiss routed; Sherman battered; Hurlbut begins defence of Hornets' Nest position.

0930 Hrs – Johnston summons Breckinridge's reserves; W.H.L. Wallace marches to Prentiss; Confederates probe Hornets' Nest.

1000 Hrs – Grant and Sherman consult; McClernand's line overwhelmed; assaults against Hornets' Nest begin.

1100 Hrs – Johnston to the right flank; Bragg assumes tactical control of assaults against Hornets' Nest.

1400 Hrs – Confederate right wing outflanks Hornets' Nest.

1430 Hrs – Jordan commits last reserves; Johnston dies; Bowen, Jackson and Chalmers envelope Hornets' Nest.

1500 Hrs – Ruggles begins to assemble grand battery; Union right retires to final defensive line.

1700 Hrs – Prentiss surrenders; Nelson reaches Landing.

1730 Hrs – Last Confederate charge repulsed at Landing.

1915 Hrs – Lew Wallace's Division reaches the field.

7 April

0500 Hrs – Nelson advances.

0600 Hrs – Buell halts Nelson.

0800 Hrs – Federal assault at standstill; Confederate line stabilised.

0900 Hrs – Combined Federal armies advance.

1000 Hrs – Hardee counterattacks Buell.

1300 Hrs – Hard fighting in front of Shiloh Church.

1400 Hrs – Confederate line dissolves.

1430 Hrs – Beauregard orders retreat.

1600 Hrs – Confederate rearguard retires.

7 April – Pope captures Island No. 10 on Mississippi.
8 April – Forrest repulses pursuing Federals.
25 April – In the absence of the men sent to Shiloh, New Orleans falls.
30 April – Halleck begins slow advance on Corinth; Grant kicked upstairs as second-in-command.
29 May – Beauregard evacuates Corinth.
10 June – Having massed 120,000 men at Corinth, Halleck unwisely disperses them, thereby missing a great opportunity.
June – Halleck summoned to Washington to become Colonel-in-chief; Grant reinstated.
27 June – After Beauregard goes on unauthorised sick leave, Bragg assumes command of Army of Tennessee.

1863
4 July – Vicksburg surrenders to Grant.
19-20 September – Battle of Chickamauga.
17 October – Grant assumes control of all important US forces west of the Allegheny Mountains.
25 November – Grant wins battle of Chattanooga.
28 November – Bragg asks to be relieved of command.

1864
30 November – Battle of Franklin where the Army of Tennessee is slaughtered.
15-16 December – Battle of Nashville routs Army of Tennessee.

Five different Confederate commands contributed manpower in order to achieve the concentration of force necessary to challenge Grant's army. The camp of the 3rd Kentucky in Corinth before the battle. The typical lack of uniforms made many rebel regiments look like a mob of armed citizens. (Library of Congress)

OPPOSING COMMANDERS

THE CONFEDERATE GENERALS

During the Mexican War, Sidney Johnston's quick-thinking reaction to a dangerous confrontation had probably saved the lives of both himself and Jefferson Davis. Thereafter, Davis's admiration knew no bounds. The outbreak of the Civil War found Johnston posted in California. Davis appointed his friend to one of the top five ranking positions in the Confederate army, reserved an important command for him, and anxiously awaited his return back east.

Like all Civil War generals, Johnston's experience did not include commanding large numbers of men in battle. He was a big man who looked like a soldier and had a commanding, magnetic per-

General P.G.T. Beauregard served as Johnston's second-in-command. During the battle's first day he remained in the rear in order to facilitate the flow of reserves to the front. It proved a mistake since he was kept badly out of touch with front-line developments. On both days, his tactical instructions were to head for the sounds of the heaviest firing and engage. (National Archives)

sonality. However, when Johnston's defence of Tennessee collapsed in the late winter of 1862, the Tennessee congressional delegation asked the president to remove Johnston from command, saying he was 'no general'. Davis replied that if Johnston was not a general, 'we had better give up the war, for we have no general'. The field at Shiloh would test this belief.

Johnston's deputy, Gen. Beauregard, did have the experience of high command under his belt. Beauregard had led the Confederate army at the war's first great battle along the banks of Bull Run and had received much credit after the victory. But the lofty Creole had quickly fallen foul of the equally proud Confederate president. Beauregard specialised in ambitious strategic constructs. When others dissented, he could become difficult and this is what occurred after the first Battle of Bull Run. The clash of strong-willed personalities had prompted Davis to rid himself of this troublesome subordinate by sending him west. Beauregard appreciated that his victory at Bull Run had been greatly aided by Maj.Gen. Joseph Johnston, who had remained in the rear where he had controlled the dispatch of reserves. In Tennessee, Beauregard resolved to emulate Joe Johnston's service.

Four rebel generals assumed corps command within the Confederate striking force. Major-General Leonidas Polk, who led the First Corps, had graduated from West Point in 1827, went on furlough, and decided to discard his military uniform for that of an Episcopal minister. Since

First Corps Commander Maj.Gen. Leonidas Polk. 'Bishop' Polk owed his rank to his friendship with Jefferson Davis. Although a West Point graduate, he lacked both military knowledge and tactical acumen. (Tennessee State Library and Archives)

Second Corps Commander Maj.Gen. Braxton Bragg. A Union prisoner met Bragg two months after the battle and found him to have 'a face rather impatient and irate in expression, a little inclined to be contemptuous, and conveys a general impression of a man who would require a great deal more of others than of himself'. (Library of Congress)

Third Corps Commander Maj.Gen. William Hardee. Confederate soldiers widely admired Hardee, judging him to be a soldier's general. (National Archives)

Reserve Corps Commander Brig.Gen. John Breckinridge. Shiloh was Breckinridge's first combat action. (Library of Congress)

that time he had neither studied war, nor commanded on a battlefield. His recent unhappy experience in Kentucky was the sum total of his field experience.

Major-General Braxton Bragg, whose strategic suggestion had contributed to the massing of the rebel force in western Tennessee, led the Second Corps. A West Point graduate, Bragg had fought in Mexico where he had performed well. But this war would show that his tactical notions were limited to the direct approach: the enemy is there, we will attack him frontally with the bayonet. Bragg also served as the army's chief of staff. It was a dual responsibility that would have overburdened anyone and contributed to the sloppy staff work that characterised the army's approach march to battle.

Major-General William Hardee commanded the Third Corps. Officers north and south believed the West Point-educated Hardee to be a fine general. In fact, Hardee's reputation resided in his authorship of a pre-war tactical manual which was little more than a translation of a French drill book, and in his service as tactics teacher at West Point. He had fought in the Seminole War, the Mexican War and had studied at the French cavalry school at Saumur. Hardee would serve in corps command throughout the war and failed to display anything beyond average talent.

In contrast, the politician who led the army's Reserve Corps, John Breckinridge, a former US vice-president, would rise to display surprising battlefield abilities. But at Shiloh, his first exposure to combat, Breckinridge deferred to the Mexican War veterans and West Point graduates who, everyone assumed, possessed superior talent.

In short, the Confederate Army of the Mississippi engaged at Shiloh under the supreme command of an officer who had never before led a sizeable force in combat; a second-in-command who had little staff experience, yet was serving as the *de facto* chief of staff; and with a corps structure that was less than a week old.

THE FEDERAL GENERALS

Across the field, the rebels confronted an army that was much the same, although there was one important difference. At this stage in the war, Ulysses S. Grant had already conducted several campaigns and fought two field battles. True enough, the battle of Belmont had been a narrowly averted disaster, and the rebel breakout attack at Fort Donelson had found Grant far from the field having failed to leave adequate instructions for his subordinates. But at that battle Grant had seen his soldiers run from the enemy and had calmly responded to crisis by rallying his men and returning them to the fray. More than any other Civil War general, he understood that even at the darkest moment the

enemy was subject to all of the problems – prominently including disorganisation, shock, and anxiety about the opponent's intentions – that afflicted his own men in battle. In his first important service in 1861, Grant had found himself confronting the severe self-doubt associated with independent command. It had been a pivotal, formative experience that taught him that the enemy 'had as much reason to fear my forces as I had his'. He had been tested, and displayed the moral courage necessary for high command.

A corps structure was late to catch on among the western Federal armies. Consequently, Grant's Army of the Tennessee featured six divisions, but no corps. Like their opponents, the command structure included political appointees such as John McClernand, an Illinois lawyer friend of Abraham Lincoln, as well as West Point graduates and Mexican War veterans who had never commanded any sizeable body of men. Surprisingly, five of the six men commanding divisions in Grant's army had not attended West Point. The exception was William T. Sherman, who had led a brigade at Bull Run and then transferred west. While serving in Kentucky, he had worried excessively that his command was about to be attacked by overwhelming force, and his anxieties led to a nervous breakdown. He lost the administration's confidence, with some saying that this man was so inept that he was certifiably insane. Reinstated, Sherman now commanded the raw Fifth Division. Whether he was worthy of divisional command was an untested proposition. Moreover, although four of the six Federal divisions included many units who had fought during the Fort Donelson campaign, the two most inexperienced divisions occupied the forward position closest to the Confederate base at Corinth.

Unlike Sidney Johnston, at Shiloh, Maj.Gen. Ulysses Grant already had campaign and battle experience. Still, he was extremely fortunate to win the battle of Shiloh. Never again did he repeat the mistakes he made on this field. (National Archives)

Sherman (seated centre left) and his principal subordinates during his Georgia campaign. Two Shiloh veterans are present: Logan, seated to Sherman's right, who rose from regimental command at Shiloh to command briefly the Army of the Tennessee before returning to corps command; and Hazen, standing on Sherman's right, who reached divisional command. At Shiloh, Sherman had three horses shot out from under him, a nearby aide killed, a buckshot wound to the hand, and a spent ball strike his shoulder. (Library of Congress)

OPPOSING ARMIES

The volunteer regiments that made up most of the Federal fighting force had no battalion structure. Instead they featured ten companies (a legacy of the nation's British military heritage), with overall command exercised by a colonel, a lieutenant-colonel, and a major. A captain commanded each company, supported by a first and a second lieutenant, one first sergeant, four sergeants, and eight corporals. This assembly led 82 privates. An average volunteer regiment went to the front with about 1,000 men. Attrition quickly reduced strengths to 200 to 300 men. The volunteer regiment's ten companies were lettered according to their captains' seniority. Again in keeping with British tradition, two companies – A and B – served as semi-élite flank companies. Company A had pride of place on the right, since this was the position that would meet danger first when the regiment marched by the right flank. Company B stood on the left flank. Often, particularly early in the war, the flank companies received superior weapons and performed hazardous duties.

The typical regiment comprised companies raised from the same community and regiments recruited from the same region. Thus friendship, kinship, and shared backgrounds and values knitted a unit together. The soldiers elected their officers, which could cause problems because the best stump speaker or most liberal dispenser of pre-election whisky might not prove the most able tactical leader. Still, this democratic system did mean that the men knew their officers and were more likely to respect their orders than if a total stranger had been imposed upon them. Because the battle of Shiloh quickly degenerated into a

A western Federal division in battle formation: from front to back, individual skirmishers, a squad (lying down) as picket supports, a company (lying down) as picket reserve, three battle lines with artillery support on the flanks, and a reserve brigade in right rear. Maintaining command and control of a linear formation in Shiloh's tangled terrain proved impossible. (Author's collection)

small unit brawl, the performance of field-grade officers would be particularly important.

During the war's earliest battles, the regiment was the largest tactical entity. As armies grew larger, the need for higher levels of organisation became apparent. This led to the formation of brigades and divisions. Nominally, a brigadier-general led a brigade, but at Shiloh many colonels actually commanded the combat brigades. By US War Department order, and unlike the Confederate practice, there was no effort to create brigades composed of regiments from the same state. Most of Grant's infantry brigades at Shiloh had four or five regiments. Sherman's raw division was still forming and consequently his under-strength brigades had only three regiments.

The US War Department decreed on 3 August 1861 that three brigades would form a division, and each division would be led by a major-general. Few Federal soldiers felt any particular attachment to whichever division their regiment was assigned. For their officers, however, the division structure greatly eased the problems of command and control. At the battle of Belmont, Grant had issued orders to individual regiments. In his next campaign against Fort Donelson, he was no longer concerned with individual regiments, but instead thought in terms of divisions. From the Federal command viewpoint, the battle of Shiloh was a divisional battle.

From a practical standpoint, this meant Grant had to control the field through the five divisional commanders who were present when the rebel attack began. The lack of a higher corps structure impaired co-ordination. One division might hold hard while the two adjacent divisions would (and did!) retreat, exposing the tenacious division to attack in the flank. Instead, if the divisions had been bound by a corps-level attachment, there would have been greater harmony of manoeuvre.

Regular cavalry regiments had three battalions of two squadrons each, and two companies made up a squadron. By regulation, each company included a captain, first lieutenant, second lieutenant, first sergeant, a company quartermaster-sergeant, four sergeants, eight corporals, two musicians (usually buglers), two farriers, a saddler, a wagoner, and 56 privates. The fact that 12 sergeants and corporals were deemed necessary to manage 56 cavalry privates (the same number of non-commissioned officers who controlled 82 infantry privates) indicates that authorities recognised that a mounted man required more control than his foot-slogging brethren. The battalion featured 316 company officers and men, along with a major, an adjutant, quartermaster/commissary lieutenant, sergeant-major, quartermaster-sergeant, commissary sergeant, hospital steward, saddler sergeant, and a veterinary sergeant giving a total minimum strength of 325 men. The regiment added a colonel, lieutenant-colonel, adjutant, quartermaster and commissary lieutenant, two chief buglers, and a 16-man band. The volunteer cavalry regiments consisted of four to six squadrons, with each squadron having two companies. At Shiloh the Union cavalry had yet to form into a brigade structure. Instead, they served as independent battalions and regiments under the direct command of the divisional general.

The battery was the basic field artillery unit. Its minimum authorised composition included a captain, first lieutenant, second lieutenant, first sergeant, company quartermaster sergeant, four sergeants, eight corporals, two musicians, two artificers, one wagoner, and 58 privates. As was the case with the cavalry, the authorities recognised that the artillery, the most technical of the three branches of service, needed a greater proportion of non-commissioned officer control than did the infantry. A field artillery battery had four or six artillery tubes, which were a combination of guns and howitzers. Volunteer artillery regiments had a 12-battery organisation, with each battery containing 144 officers and men. The artillery's regimental structure was purely an administrative convention.

Although the Union batteries had informal associations with specific infantry brigades, like the cavalry they operated independ-ently under the command of the divisional commander. This was a flawed organisational practice. Too often a harassed infantry division general overlooked his artillery, thus leaving the gunners who served Grant's 84 artillery pieces to perform as best as they could.

Overall, Grant's army included a variety of units who had only recently reached Pittsburg Landing. The 15th

The 11th Indiana, a well-trained Zouave unit, served in Lew Wallace's division. Camp recreation scenes at top; middle-left, deployed as skirmishers; middle right, rallying by fours; bottom, formed in hollow square. The civilian spectators in lower right admire the square, but in reality it proved wholly unnecessary on the battlefield. (Library of Congress)

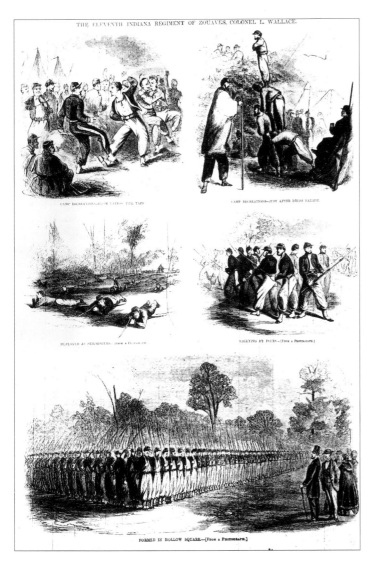

THE ELEVENTH INDIANA REGIMENT OF ZOUAVES, COLONEL L. WALLACE.

CAMP RECREATIONS—FROM TATTOO TILL TAPS.

CAMP RECREATIONS—JUST AFTER DRESS PARADE.

DEPLOYED AS SKIRMISHERS.—[FROM A PHOTOGRAPH.]

RALLYING BY FOURS.—[FROM A PHOTOGRAPH.]

FORMED IN HOLLOW SQUARE.—[FROM A PHOTOGRAPH.]

Iowa actually arrived for duty on Sunday morning after the fighting had begun. On the day of battle many had not the time to establish cohesive links with their fellow units and some 2,000 men had yet to be assigned to any particular command.

The Confederate forces

Confederate small unit infantry organisation differed little from Federal organisation, the only difference being that infantry companies nominally numbered 64 to 100 men. The Army of the Mississippi had been hastily formed from disparate units so there was hardly a typical brigade organisation. The infantry brigades numbered four to eight regiments or battalions, and all had one or two attached artillery batteries. Unlike their opponents, the Confederates employed a corps structure. Polk's First and Bragg's Second Corps had two divisions each, but neither Hardee's Third, nor Breckinridge's Reserve Corps had a division structure. Like the Yankees, the rebel cavalry had yet to form into a brigade structure. Instead, autonomous companies, battalions, and regiments operated directly under corps command.

Confederate artillery contained 23 batteries, one-third possessing four guns, and two-thirds with six guns, while Byrne's Mississippi Battery proudly carried a piece captured in Kentucky and thus composed a seven-gun battery. Eighty-five per cent of the tubes were smoothbore 6-pdrs. and 12-pdr. howitzers, inferior weapons at a disadvantage in long-range artillery duels. Most of the gunners had never seen action and some had yet to fire their pieces. Their ranks did include some notable formations, such as Girardey's Washington Artillery, a well-trained six-gun battery from Augusta, Georgia; Ketchum's and Gage's Alabama batteries drawn from the cream of Mobile society; and the renowned Washington Artillery from Louisiana. Like the Federal artillery, the batteries were attached to infantry brigades. The three line corps had a nominal chief of artillery,

The 9th Mississippi at Pensacola. The diversity of dress is already evident with the men at left and middle proudly displaying cart-ridge belts with buckles and shoulder straps. The man kneeling over the fire, and the soldier at far right are possibly brothers since both are wearing the same pattern checked trousers. The obviously wealthy man second from right has a splendid civilian frock coat, waistcoat, and top hat. At Shiloh the 9th Mississippi served in Chalmers' Brigade. (Library of Congress)

OPPOSITE **A Confederate infantryman in regulation issue uniform. Shiloh was the first combat for many regiments, and the standard of dress was higher than the campaign-stained look that characterised western armies thereafter. (National Archives)**

ABOVE **Alabama infantry at Pensacola. Soldiers from the Gulf coast defences took the train to join the Army of the Mississippi at Corinth. (Library of Congress)**

but in fact the officers assigned this duty had no real authority. Thus the first stages of the battle would see one officer wasting his time gathering up captured Union equipment, while another relinquished his position to direct his own battery. The battery to brigade assignments, as well as the lack of supervising artillery commanders, impaired effective use of massed firepower.

Neither side was well armed at this stage of the war. Hardee's Corps had 6,789 infantry, most of whom carried smoothbore muskets. Some 1,060 men had Enfield rifles, but there were only 31,000 cartridges. Since prolonged fire fights easily consumed 40 to 60 rounds per man, this meant that Hardee's rifle-armed soldiers entered battle woefully under-supplied with ammunition.

Shiloh would be a terrifying, stand-up battle between two civilian armies. Many soldiers would be crushed by the strain. They feigned sickness before entering combat, shammed wounds, lay down in shelter once the bullets began whizzing and refused to budge, or ran at first contact. However, many more would perform admirably. What motivated them to confront the horrors of battle? Peer pressure was most important. Aligned in close order formation, a man could hardly duck his duty without being noticed. Shirking was highly visible, and a coward was roundly criticised by his comrades and reported to the people back home. For many, such a fate was worse than risking life and limb in battle. The determination not to let down one's comrades provided the glue that cemented the inexperienced soldier to his duty.

The Union soldiers of 1862 had volunteered for service out of a sense of patriotism and spirit of adventure. The link between the community and the regiment was strong. The 16th Iowa, a typical regiment, entered the fight with the motto 'Keep up the good name of Iowa'.

The same motives influenced the Confederate soldiers. However, for them it was also a matter of defending their homeland from an invader. A speech by a young woman, given during a ceremony presenting the flag to a Louisiana unit, was altogether typical: 'Receive then, from your mothers and sisters...these colors woven by our feeble but reliant hands; and when this bright flag shall float before you on the battlefield, let it not only inspire you with the brave and patriotic ambition of a soldier aspiring to his own and his country's honor and glory, but also may it be a sign that cherished ones appeal to you to save them from a fanatical and heartless foe.'

19

ORDER OF BATTLE

ABBREVIATIONS

Abbreviations of rank:
Maj Gen =Major General, **Lt Gen**=Lieutenant-General,
Brig. Gen =Brigadier General, **Col** =Colonel,
Lt Col.=Lieutenant Colonel, **Maj**=Major, **Cpt**=Captain,
1st Lt=1st Lt, and **2nd Lt**=2nd Lieutenant.

CONFEDERATE TROOPS AT SHILOH
Regiments By State

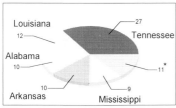

* Kentucky, 5;
Texas, 2; CSA,
2; Florida, 1;
Missouri, 1

ARMY OF THE MISSISSIPPI

Commander: Gen. Albert Sidney Johnston
Second-in-Command: Gen. P.G.T. Beauregard
(41,222 total)

FIRST CORPS

Maj.Gen. Leonidas Polk (9,404)

FIRST DIVISION

Brig.Gen. Charles Clark

FIRST BRIGADE
Col. Robert Russell
11th Louisiana
12th Tennessee
13th Tennessee
22nd Tennessee
Bankhead's Tennessee Batt.

SECOND BRIGADE
Brig.Gen. Alexander Stewart
13th Arkansas
4th Tennessee
5th Tennessee
33rd Tennessee
Stanford's Mississippi Batt.

SECOND DIVISION

Maj.Gen. Benjamin Cheatham

FIRST BRIGADE
Brig.Gen. Bushrod Johnson
Blythe's Mississippi Bn.
2nd Tennessee
15th Tennessee
154th Tennessee (senior)
Polk's Tennessee Batt.

SECOND BRIGADE
Col. William Stephens
7th Kentucky
1st Tennessee Bn.
6th Tennessee
9th Tennessee
Smith's Mississippi Batt.

CAVALRY
1st Mississippi Cavalry
Brewer's Mississippi and Alabama Bn.

SECOND CORPS

Maj.Gen. Braxton Bragg (16,279)
Escort Smith's Alabama Cavalry (company)

FIRST DIVISION

Brig.Gen. Daniel Ruggles

FIRST BRIGADE
Col. Randall Gibson
1st Arkansas
4th Louisiana
13th Louisiana
19th Louisiana
Bains' Mississippi Batt. (left in Corinth)

SECOND BRIGADE
Brig.Gen. Patton Anderson
1st Florida (Bn.)
17th Louisiana
20th Louisiana
9th Texas
Confederate Guards Response Bn.
Washington Louisiana Artillery, 5th Company
(Hodgson's Batt.)

THIRD BRIGADE
Col. Preston Pond
16th Louisiana
18th Louisiana
Crescent (Louisiana) Regiment
Orleans Guard Bn.
38th Tennessee
Ketchum's Alabama Batt.

CAVALRY
Alabama Bn. (five companies)

SECOND DIVISION

Brig.Gen. Jones Withers

FIRST BRIGADE
Brig.Gen. Adley Gladden
21st Alabama
22nd Alabama
25th Alabama
26th Alabama
1st Louisiana
Robertson's Florida Batt.

SECOND BRIGADE
Brig.Gen. James Chalmers
5th Mississippi
7th Mississippi
9th Mississippi
10th Mississippi
52nd Tennessee
Gage's Alabama Batt.

THIRD BRIGADE
Brig.Gen. John Jackson
17th Alabama
18th Alabama
19th Alabama
2nd Texas
Girardey's Georgia
Washington Artillery

CAVALRY
Clanton's Alabama Rangers

Note: 47th Tennessee arrived on field on 7 April

THIRD CORPS

Maj.Gen. William Hardee (6,758)

FIRST BRIGADE
Brig.Gen. Thomas Hindman
2nd Arkansas
6th Arkansas
7th Arkansas
3rd Confederate
Miller's Tennessee Batt.
(Pillow's Flying Artillery)
Swett's Mississippi Batt.
(Warren Light Artillery)

SECOND BRIGADE
Brig.Gen. Patrick Cleburne
15th Arkansas
6th Mississippi
5th [35] Tennessee
23rd Tennessee
24th Tennessee
2nd Tennessee
Shop's Artillery Bn. (Trill's Arkansas, Culvert's
    Arkansas, and Hubbard's Arkansas Batteries)
Watson's Louisiana Batt. (detached at Grand
    Junction)

THIRD BRIGADE
Brig.Gen. Sterling Wood
16th Alabama
8th Arkansas
9th Arkansas Bn.
3rd Mississippi Bn.
27th Tennessee
44th Tennessee
55th Tennessee
Harper's (Jefferson Mississippi) Flying
    Artillery
Georgia Dragoons
(one company)

RESERVE CORPS

Brig.Gen. John Breckinridge (7,211)

FIRST BRIGADE
Col. Robert Trabue
4th Alabama Bn.
31st Alabama
3rd Kentucky
4th Kentucky
5th Kentucky
6th Kentucky
Crews' Tennessee Bn.
Byrne's Kentucky Batt.
Cobb's Kentucky Batt.
Morgan's Squadron
Kentucky Cavalry

SECOND BRIGADE
Brig.Gen. John Bowen
9th Arkansas
10th Arkansas
2nd Confederate
1st Missouri
Pettus Flying Artillery
(Hudson's Mississippi Batt.)
Thompson's Company
Kentucky Cavalry,

THIRD BRIGADE
Col. Winfield Statham
15th Mississippi
22nd Mississippi
19th Tennessee
20th Tennessee
28th Tennessee
45th Tennessee
Rutledge's Tennessee Batt.
Forrest's Regiment Tennessee Cavalry

UNASSIGNED
Wharton's Texas Rangers (cavalry)
Adam's Mississippi Regiment (cavalry)
McClung's Tennessee Batt.
Robert's Arkansas Batt.
(Cavalry total: 4,316)

ARMY OF THE TENNESSEE AT SHILOH
Regiments By State

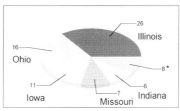

Illinois 26
Ohio 16
Iowa 11
Missouri 7
Indiana 6
8 *

* Wisconsin, 3;
Kentucky, 2;
Michigan, 2,
and Nebraska, 1

ARMY OF THE TENNESSEE

Maj.Gen. Ulysses S. Grant (46,710)

FIRST DIVISION

Maj.Gen. John A. McClernand (6,941)

FIRST BRIGADE
Col. Abraham M. Hare
8th Illinois
18th Illinois
11th Iowa
13th Iowa
2nd Illinois Lt. Artillery, Batt. D

SECOND BRIGADE
Col. C. Carroll Marsh
11th Illinois
20th Illinois
45th Illinois
48th Illinois

THIRD BRIGADE
Col. Julius Raith
17th Illinois
29th Illinois
43rd Illinois
49th Illinois
Illinois Cavalry Co.

UNATTACHED
Stewart's Co. Illinois Cavalry
1st Illinois Lt. Artillery, Batt. A
2nd Illinois Lt. Artillery, Batt. E
Ohio Lt. Artillery, 14th Batt.

SECOND DIVISION

Brig.Gen. William H.L. Wallace (8,408)

FIRST BRIGADE
Col. James M. Tuttle
2nd Iowa
7th Iowa
12th Iowa
14th Iowa

SECOND BRIGADE
Brig.Gen. John McArthur
9th Illinois
12th Illinois
13th Missouri
14th Missouri
81st Ohio

THIRD BRIGADE
Col. Thomas W. Sweeny
8th Iowa
7th Illinois
50th Illinois
52nd Illinois
57th Illinois
58th Illinois

CAVALRY
2nd Illinois, Co. A & B
2nd US, Co. C
4th US, Co. I

ARTILLERY
1st Illinois Lt., Batt. A
1st Missouri Lt., Batt. D, H, K

THIRD DIVISION

Maj.Gen. Lewis Wallace (7,564)

FIRST BRIGADE
Col. Morgan L. Smith
11th Indiana
24th Indiana
8th Missouri

SECOND BRIGADE
Col. John M. Thayer
23rd Indiana
1st Nebraska
58th Ohio
68th Ohio

THIRD BRIGADE
Col. Charles Whittlesey
20th Ohio
56th Ohio
76th Ohio
78th Ohio

ARTILLERY
Indiana Lt., 9th Batt.
1st Missouri Lt., Batt. I

CAVALRY
11th Illinois, 3rd Bn.
5th Ohio, 3rd Bn.

FOURTH DIVISION

Brig.Gen. Stephen A. Hurlbut (7,825)

FIRST BRIGADE
Col. Nelson G. Williams
28th Illinois
32nd Illinois
41st Illinois
3rd Iowa

SECOND BRIGADE
Col. James C. Veatch
14th Illinois
15th Illinois
46th Illinois
25th Indiana

THIRD BRIGADE
Brig.Gen. Jacob G. Lauman
31st Indiana
44th Indiana
17th Kentucky
25th Kentucky

CAVALRY
5th Ohio, 1st & 2nd Bns.
ARTILLERY
Michigan Light, 2nd Batt.
Missouri Light, Mann's Batt.
Ohio Light, 13th Batt.

FIFTH DIVISION

Brig.Gen. William T. Sherman (8,580)

FIRST BRIGADE
Col. John A. McDowell
40th Illinois
6th Iowa
46th Ohio
Indiana Light Artillery, 6th Batt.

SECOND BRIGADE
Col. David Stuart
55th Illinois
54th Ohio
71st Ohio

THIRD BRIGADE
Col. Jesse Hildebrand
53rd Ohio
57th Ohio
77th Ohio

FOURTH BRIGADE
Col. Ralph P. Buckland
48th Ohio
70th Ohio
72nd Ohio

CAVALRY
4th Illinois, 1st & 2nd Bns.

ARTILLERY
Maj. Ezra Taylor
1st Illinois Light, Batt. B & E

SIXTH DIVISION

Brig.Gen. Benjamin M. Prentiss (7,545)

FIRST BRIGADE
Col. Everett Peabody
12th Michigan
21st Missouri
25th Missouri
16th Wisconsin

SECOND BRIGADE
Col. Madison Miller
61st Illinois
16th Iowa
18th Missouri

CAVALRY
11th Illinois (8 companies)

ARTILLERY
Minnesota Light, 1st Batt.
Ohio Light, 5th Batt.

UNATTACHED INFANTRY
15th Iowa
23rd Missouri
18th Wisconsin

UNASSIGNED TROOPS (2,031)
15th Michigan
14th Wisconsin
1st Illinois Light Artillery, Batt. H & Batt. I
2nd Illinois Light Artillery, Batt. B & Batt. F
Ohio Light Artillery, 8th Batt.

ARMY OF THE OHIO

Maj.Gen. Don Carlos Buell

FIFTH DIVISION

Brig.Gen. Thomas Crittenden (3,825)

ELEVENTH BRIGADE
Brig.Gen. Jeremiah Boyle
9th Kentucky
13th Kentucky
19th Ohio
59th Ohio

FOURTEENTH BRIGADE
Col. William Smith
11th Kentucky
26th Kentucky
13th Ohio

ARTILLERY
Bartlett's Batt. G, 1st Ohio Lt. Artillery
Mendenhall's Batts. H & M, 4th US

SECOND DIVISION

Brig.Gen. Alexander McCook (7,552)

FOURTH BRIGADE
Brig.Gen. Lovell Rousseau
6th Indiana
5th Kentucky
1st Ohio
1/15th US
1/16th US
1/19th US

FIFTH BRIGADE
Col. Edward Kirk
34th Illinois
29th Indiana
30th Indiana
77th Pennsylvania

SIXTH BRIGADE
Col. William Gibson
32nd Indiana
39th Indiana
15th Ohio
49th Ohio

ARTILLERY
Terrill's Batt. H, 5th US

FOURTH DIVISION

Brig.Gen. William Nelson (4,541)

TENTH BRIGADE
Col. Jacob Ammen
36th Indiana
6th Ohio
25th Ohio

NINETEENTH BRIGADE
Col. William Hazen
9th Indiana
6th Kentucky
41st Ohio

TWENTY-SECOND BRIGADE
Col. Sanders Bruce
1st Kentucky
2nd Kentucky
20th Kentucky

SIXTH DIVISION

Brig.Gen. Thomas Wood (2,000)
(arrived 2 pm, 7 April)

TWENTIETH BRIGADE
Brig.Gen. James Garfield
13th Michigan
64th Ohio
65th Ohio

TWENTY-FIRST BRIGADE
Col. George Wagner
15th Indiana
50th Indiana
57th Indiana
24th Kentucky

OPPOSING PLANS

APPROACH MARCH, 3-5 APRIL 1862

Overcoming poor roads and sloppy staff work, Johnston's army manages a 23-mile approach march and deploys for battle. Because of poor camp security, the Union army is taken by surprise.

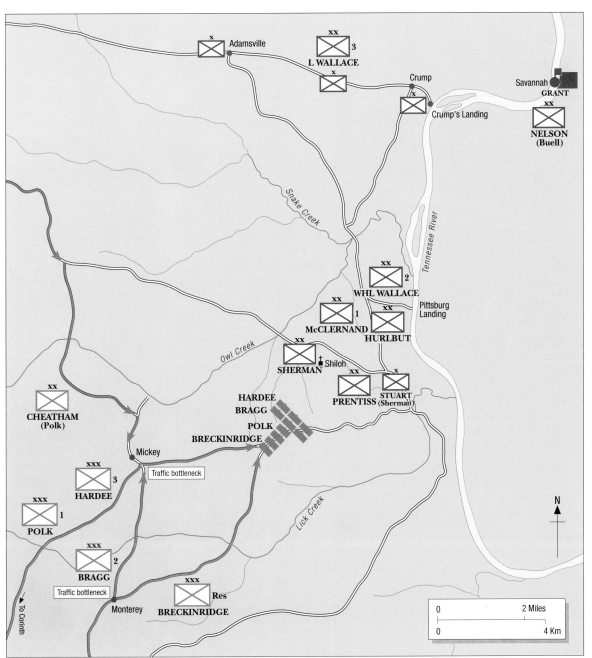

Grant's army encamped at Pittsburg Landing in a triangular area bounded by water. The army's rear rested on the Tennessee River, with the left flank on Lick Creek and the right against Snake Creek and Owl Creek. The Tennessee provided a solid barrier passable only by boat, and the creeks were passable only at the bridges. The open, or western, side of the position faced toward Corinth. In effect, the Union army was in a cul-de-sac, and their camps were positioned for convenience without tactical thought. Except for the cleared fields, trees and underbrush covered the land, making much of it impassable for wheeled transport, artillery, and horsemen. The ground was without significant elevations. It generally sloped down from the most forward Yankee positions back toward the Tennessee River. A steep bluff ran along the west bank of the Tennessee River, and was bisected by an improved path that climbed up from the landing. Here stood the Army of the Tennessee, perfecting its drill, adding to its organisation, waiting for Buell's reinforcements to arrive before resuming active campaigning.

Twenty-three road miles separated the Confederate encampment at Corinth from the Union tents around Pittsburg Landing. As might be expected given the inexperience of the Army of the Mississippi, the Confederate approach march was a miserable, start-stop-start affair. Poor, rain-soaked roads and inadequate staff work contributed to the disorder. Columns fouled one another's line of march, overloaded baggage trains bogged down in the mud, guides became lost. Polluted water at Corinth had weakened the bowels of many rebels (the army left a staggering 7,645 sick back at base). Individuals started the march with rations for five days and in typical soldier style lightened their load by eating them in three. Thus hunger and the failure of the supply wagons to keep up, coupled with exposure to rain and wind, weakened them further. Before attempting to sleep, one soldier wrote in his diary, 'More heavy rain! Hard going, had to abandon light baggage. Again marched more than 12 hrs'.

In the belief that Beauregard better understood local conditions, Johnston allowed his second-in-command to draft battle plans. Beauregard's scheme called for the attack to commence on 4 April. When that proved impossible, Johnston delayed it by 24 hours. After waiting on the edge of the Union camps for an additional four hours past the designated start time, and still not hearing the sounds of battle, Sidney Johnston stormed, 'This is perfectly puerile! This is not war!' Generals Bragg, Polk, Beauregard and Johnston met to decide what to do. Convinced that surprise had been lost, Beauregard urged a retreat. Displaying great soldierly resolve, Johnston overrode him. He desired battle, and did not care about the details. Referring to the fact that the battle front would be constricted by Owl

A rakish Louisiana soldier with baggy trousers and gaiters. While 12 regiments of Louisiana soldiers fought at Shiloh, New Orleans, the South's largest city, fell to a small naval landing team 18 days later. (National Archives)

At 5:00 am Maj. Powell led his combat patrol into this field where stood the 3rd Mississippi Infantry Battalion. The ensuing fire fight began the battle of Shiloh. (Author's collection)

and Lick Creeks, Johnston confided to an aide, 'I would fight them if they were a million. They can present no greater front between these two creeks than we can.'

According to Gen. Beauregard's deployment scheme, the army would form three corps-sized lines stretching between Owl and Lick Creeks, with a central reserve of three brigades. Hardee's Corps deployed into battle formation to compose the first line, with its artillery massed along the main road to the landing and its cavalry in support of the wings. Since these were not enough men to cover the entire front, Gladden's Brigade from Bragg's Corps advanced to take up a position on Hardee's right. Bragg's remaining five brigades deployed into battle line 500 yards behind Hardee. Eight hundred yards behind Bragg stood Polk's Corps. Unlike the more advanced corps, it remained in a line of brigade columns with the batteries stationed behind each of the four columns. Breckinridge's three brigades also formed brigade column and brought up the rear. Thus the rebel army had nine brigades deployed for immediate action, with seven more in column to support the front.

The army's assistant adjutant-general would later boast how he modelled the deployment upon that used by Napoleon at Waterloo. In open European terrain it might have served, but in Shiloh's tangled terrain it was badly inappropriate. The army's initial position lay at the base of a funnel with a frontage of about three miles. The front would double as the army advanced. Thus, each of the leading three corps commanders would have to attempt to control the action across an extensive and expanding front, where his line of sight would typically be restricted by the woods to one or two hundred yards. In the resultant command void, a Confederate staff officer, Col. Thomas Jordan, would make critical tactical decisions. Distributing manpower evenly across the entire front also meant that there was no concentration of force. Moreover, lost amidst the linear dispersion was the essence of Johnston's plan: to turn Grant's left flank 'so as to cut off his line of retreat to the Tennessee River and throw him back on Owl Creek, where he will be obliged to surrender'. The Confederate disposition failed to provide the necessary extra strength on the army's right flank to accomplish this.

Civil War generals tried to emulate Napoleon by issuing eve of battle proclamations. Sidney Johnston told his army: 'I have put you in motion to offer battle to the invaders of your country. With the resolution and disciplined valour becoming men fighting...you can but march to a decisive victory over the agrarian mercenaries sent to subjugate and despoil you... The eyes and hopes of eight million people rest upon you.'

Across the lines, on the eve of battle, Grant, like his foes, had committed a host of errors. The difference was that his mistakes threatened his army's destruction. He had selected his position at Pittsburg Landing because its road net offered a springboard for a march on the Confederate base at Corinth. He never considered that the reverse was equally true, that Albert Sidney Johnston's army could use the same roads to advance on the Union army, and Grant failed to order his camp fortified. He had three veteran divisions, commanded by W.H.L. Wallace, Lew Wallace, and McClernand (veterans by the standards of 1862 in that they and their officers had already participated in battle), yet placed his most inexperienced divisions commanded by Sherman and Benjamin Prentiss closest to the enemy. He maintained his own

ON THE ROAD TO SHILOH
Twenty-three road miles separated the two armies' encampments, which had to be covered by the Confederates during torrential downpours. Poor road conditions and inept staff planning made it a miserable journey for all concerned and resulted in the attack being delayed by twenty-four hours.

headquarters nine miles away from the army in the comfortable town of Savannah, and omitted to nominate a divisional general for overall field command, so each division would fight without co-ordination. Lastly, neither he nor his lieutenants, particularly Sherman, took routine security precautions such as patrolling the roads between the Union camps and the enemy. On the night of 5 April Grant telegraphed Halleck, 'I have scarcely the faintest idea of an attack (general one) being made upon us.'

Quite simply, when the rebel assault came, it was a colossal surprise. At 6 am on Sunday 6 April, close to 40,000 Confederate soldiers supported by 123 artillery pieces caught five Federal divisions numbering some 33,000 men with 72 artillery pieces, ill-prepared in their camps.

Alan Perry

THE BATTLE

Outpost battle

No sooner had the Union army set up camp at Pittsburg Landing, than the rebel cavalry began probing its outpost line. This produced frequent alarms, with the pickets firing against enemy targets both real and imagined. Back at the tent line, officers and men alike had grown accustomed to such random firing and paid it little heed. Unconcern pervaded the higher command as well. During the period leading up to the battle, Sherman received several false reports of enemy presence. Such reports, coupled with the pickets' frequent wild firing, convinced the general that his soldiers had 'as much idea of war as children'. Moreover, Sherman had been relieved of command the previous autumn because of his excessive fears that his post was about to be attacked. Given a second chance here at Shiloh, he was determined not to make the same mistake.

On 4 April, the day Beauregard intended the Confederate attack to begin, a Federal detachment of the 5th Ohio Cavalry scouted some two miles toward Corinth to investigate the disappearance of a seven-man outpost. The troopers surprised the 1st Alabama Cavalry and sent them flying. Pursuing over the hill crest, the Yankees suddenly confronted a rebel battle line complete with deployed infantry and artillery. Although the Ohio cavalry did not know it, the enemy belonged to Hardee's Corps and were the vanguard of the entire Army of the Mississippi.

Returning to camp, a cavalry officer informed Sherman that a strong enemy force was present. Sherman dismissed the report saying, 'Oh – tut; tut. You militia officers get scared too easy'.

The next day featured more of the same. Some mounted men appeared on the fringes of a camp occupied by the 53rd Ohio, and the regiment's colonel, Jesse Appler, sent a patrol to investigate. The patrol exchanged shots with 'what appeared to be a picket line of men in butternut clothes', and Appler reported this incident to Sherman. Previous experience had given Sherman a low regard for the elderly, notably skittish colonel. He testily responded, 'Col. Appler. Take your damned regiment to Ohio. There is no enemy nearer than Corinth!'

So it was across the entire Union picket line. There were enough incidents to commanders to order outposts to be strengthened and to order half-hearted reconnaissance, but little more was done. Only one Federal officer seriously believed that the enemy was present. Colonel Everett Peabody commanded a brigade in Prentiss's division. He had seen action in Missouri where he displayed courage, short temper, and impetuosity. During the day of 5 April, three of his officers gave convincing reports that the enemy was near. When Peabody forwarded these reports to Prentiss, he, like Sherman, discounted them. That night Peabody could not sleep so certain was he that an attack was imminent.

Grant's men were at ease, enjoying a Sunday morning respite when the Confederate attack struck. (National Archives)

On his own initiative, without regard for the likely censure from his superiors, he ordered Maj. James Powell to take three companies of the 25th Missouri on a 3 am reconnaissance in force.

Powell was a regular army officer and efficiently gathered the unit's three best companies along with two more belonging to the 12th Michigan and set out down a wagon trail into the woods. About 5 am they entered a 40-acre clearing known as Fraley Field where some 280 men belonging to the 3rd Mississippi Infantry Battalion manned a picket line in front of Hardee's Corps. Unlike its foe, the Confederate outpost line showed alert anticipation. A cavalry vedette stood well in front of the battalion. Behind the cavalry and 200 yards in front of the battalion was a seven-man infantry outpost. Another eight-man outpost stood 100 yards further back, while pickets, deployed at 12-pace intervals, guarded both flanks. When the rebel cavalry spied Powell's men, they fired three warning shots, received a volley in return, and retired. At 90 yards range, the most advanced Confederate infantry outpost fired and fell back. Powell's men entered the field where the second outpost fired and also retired. Mid-way through Fraley Field the Federals spied a kneeling line of Mississippi soldiers apparently awaiting their approach. At 200 yards distance, impossibly long range for their smoothbores, Powell's men nervously fired another volley. The Mississippians returned the fire and one bullet struck a Missouri officer. He was the first casualty in what would become one of the bloodiest battles in American military history.

Soon thereafter, a trickle of wounded men began appearing in Peabody's camp. Peabody sent a reinforcing party of five companies belonging to the 21st Missouri to Powell's relief. Across the lines, from the time of first contact to the forward movement of the entire Confederate army, nearly 90 minutes passed. In large measure this delay was due to the rebels' inexperience. Even under ideal circumstances it took time for orders to filter down the chain of command, and the tangled thickets where the Army of the Mississippi had to deploy were far from ideal. The fact that the attack order had failed to specify a start time, instead merely urging an assault 'at the earliest time practicable', did not help. At 6:40 am, Albert Sidney Johnston mounted his charger, Fire-eater, turned to his staff, and exclaimed, 'Tonight we will water our horses in the Tennessee River.' Then he spurred Fire-eater to the front.

Hardee's assault

At Fraley Field, Maj. Powell saw the enemy battle line thicken and cavalry begin to work around his flanks. He confronted units belonging to Hardee's Corps. Hardee's men had several months' campaign ex-perience in Kentucky, but were new to pitched battle. Numbering about 7,000 men divided into three brigades, the corps included fighting officers such as Pat Cleburne, Thomas Hindman and William Bate, who were destined to rise by virtue of their merits to superior rank. Wisely, Powell decided to retire before this host. Falling back, he encountered the supports, led by Col. David Moore, whom Peabody had forwarded. Moore ignored Powell's warning and

THE CONFEDERATE PLAN IS SPRUNG

At 5 am Maj. James Powell led five companies on a recon-naissance into a 40-acre clearing known as Frealey Field. They encountered a line of cavalry vedettes who fired warning shots and withdrew to an infantry outpost line. Powell's men entered the field and approached the enemy battle line composed of the 3rd Mississippi Infantry Bat-talion. The battle of Shiloh was under way.

Moving a battery limber and caisson (note their size) through the woods was often extremely difficult, particularly when under fire and trying to manage excited horses. (National Archives)

ordered the combined force forward. They encountered Shaver's Brigade at an old cotton field known as Seay's. Rebel fire drove them back, with one round badly wounding Moore. As the Yankees recoiled from the collision, Moore's second-in-command sent word to Sherman's picket line that the enemy was present in force.

While Shaver's Brigade hesitantly worked its way forward – they were as new to their trade as their foes, and their officers had difficulty judging the strength of the opposition – Col. Peabody was eating breakfast. The muffled sounds of fighting in the Seay field prompted him to order his own brigade into line, although his actions brought down upon him the wrath of his divisional commander. Hearing the drum's long roll urgently calling the men into line, Prentiss spurred to Peabody's camp and angrily demanded if Peabody had provoked the enemy's attack by his unauthorised mission. 'Colonel Peabody,' shouted Prentiss, 'I will hold you personally responsible for bringing on this engagement.' Here was a man looking for a scapegoat!

Undaunted, Peabody led two regiments numbering about 1,100 men to the top of a nearby ravine and awaited the enemy. He encountered Powell and his men who joined his battle line. Suddenly the Confederates appeared a mere 75 yards away. Their ranks made an imposing spectacle. The colonel of the 12th Michigan wrote, 'They were visible in line, and every hill-top in the rear was covered with them'. The Union line discharged a crashing volley.

One of their targets was 19-year-old Henry Stanley, the man whose post-war search into the wilds of Africa for Doctor Livingstone would earn him undeserved fame. To Stanley it was as if a 'mountain had been upheaved, with huge rocks tumbling down a slope'. He heard a shout, 'There they are!' and the Confederate line fired back. Momentarily stunned, the rebels failed to press their attack, and instead engaged in a close-range fire fight across the ravine.

The problems of tactical co-ordination in wooded terrain now became apparent. By chance, Shaver's Brigade overlapped the Union left flank, but Peabody's right, in turn, overlapped the Confederate left. None of this could be clearly seen by the officers on the ground, however, with the result that Shaver's overlapping regiments were reluctant to advance until those on the brigade's left advanced with them. But the left flank regiments experienced great difficulty in advancing into the fierce Yankee fire.

Wood's Brigade, advancing on Shaver's left, had tried to maintain its alignment with Shaver, but found an ever-increasing gap separating them. Four of Wood's regiments veered off toward Shaver, while the remaining three continued straight ahead toward Sherman's camp. Additionally, because of the rugged terrain, Hardee's artillery, which had formed up in battery column behind the infantry brigades, had trouble keeping up with the infantry. Recent heavy rains caused wheels to bog down in the ravine bottoms, while the thick underbrush forced gunners to hack paths in order to advance. At first contact Hardee's Corps lost much of its artillery support as well as brigade and sometimes even regimental integrity, with some units attacking Prentiss's position and others assaulting Sherman.

Although Sherman would claim in both his after action report and in his *Memoirs* that his division was in line of battle when the Confederates struck, this was not the case. An officer in his 53rd Ohio relates that the men were attending to their normal Sunday morning duties: 'Officers' servants and company cooks were preparing breakfast, sen-

The scene of Shiloh Church well depicts the combination of dense thickets and open fields that characterised the battle's terrain. (Library of Congress)

SITUATION APPROXIMATELY 9 AM, 6 APRIL 1862

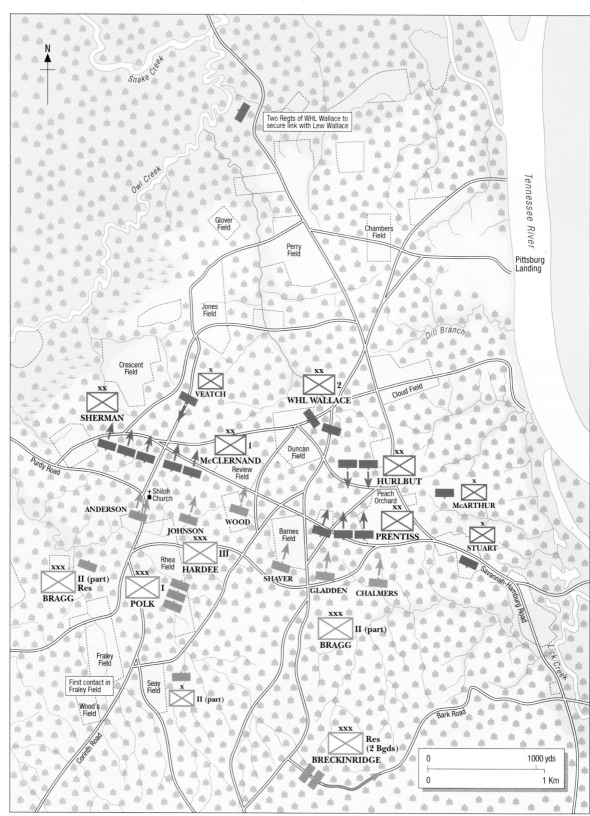

Snake Creek

Owl Creek

Tennessee River

Two Regts of WHL Wallace to
secure link with Lew Wallace

Glover
Field

Chambers
Field

Perry
Field

Pittsburg
Landing

Jones
Field

Dill Branch

Crescent
Field

Cloud Field

x
VEATCH

xx
WHL WALLACE 2

xx
SHERMAN

Purdy Road

xx
McCLERNAND I

Duncan
Field

Review
Field

xx
HURLBUT

+ Shiloh
■ Church

Peach
Orchard

x
McARTHUR

ANDERSON

WOOD

Barnes
Field

xx
PRENTISS

JOHNSON

x
STUART

xxx
HARDEE III

Rhea
Field

SHAVER

GLADDEN CHALMERS

Savannah-Hamburg Road

xxx
BRAGG II (part)
Res

xxx
POLK I

Lick Creek

xxx
BRAGG II (part)

Fraley
Field

First contact in
Fraley Field

Seay
Field

x
II (part)

Bark Road

Wood's
Field

Corinth Road

xxx
Res
(2 Bgds)
BRECKINRIDGE

| 0 | 1000 yds |
| 0 | 1 Km |

34

tinels were pacing their beats, details for brigade guard and fatigue duty were marching to their posts, and...the sutler shop was open.'

Sherman appeared at his camp line about 7 am. Accompanied by his staff, he calmly gazed through his field glass at an unknown force about half a mile distant. He did not see Confederate skirmishers advancing out of the brush only 50 yards away. A Union officer shouted to him to look to his right. Turning, Sherman saw a line of riflemen with weapons aimed directly at him. He said, 'My God, we are attacked!' The rebels fired, hitting Sherman in the hand and killing his cavalry orderly. Before galloping off to organise a defence, Sherman shouted to the man he had almost dismissed the previous day: 'Appler, hold your position; I will support you.'

Twice the rebels came to within 50 yards of Appler's position, only to recoil from the Federal fire. When the attackers came on a third time, Appler disobeyed Sherman's order and shouted out, 'Fall back and save yourselves!' The ensuing stampede partially collapsed Sherman's position. War correspondent Whitelaw Reid described the surprise rebel attack: 'Some, particularly among our officers, were not yet out of bed. Others were dressing, others washing, others cooking, a few eating their breakfasts. Many guns were unloaded, accoutrements lying pell-mell, ammunition was ill-supplied – in short, the camps were virtually surprised.'

A surviving soldier confirms Reid's account: 'Shells were hurtling through the tent...before there was time for thought or preparation,

there came rushing through the woods the line of battle sweeping the front of the division camps'. At the forefront of the rebel attack were gallant officers determined to prove themselves under fire. None surpassed Maj. J.T. Harris of the 15th Arkansas. He rode in front of his brigade's skirmish line to within pistol range of the foe, fired his revolver, and shouted to his men to come on. Then enemy musketry killed him.

Confronted with such implacable opponents, the Union position rapidly became desperate. Senior officers' official reports are seldom models of candour. Yet Sherman's after-action report does give some indication of the panic that overcame many of his units. Sherman wrote that about an hour after the Confederate assault began, 'Appler's regiment broke in disorder, soon followed by fugitives from Mungen's regiment'. Then, when the colonel of the 43rd Illinois received a severe wound and fell from his horse, 'his regiment and the others manifested disorder, and the enemy got possession of three guns'. Sherman rode to Behr's Battery to send it into action but Behr 'was almost immediately shot from his horse...the drivers and gunners fled in disorder, carrying off the caissons and abandoning five out of six guns without firing a shot'. Although much would be made of how many men ran, on balance the raw division acquitted itself well. It entered battle with 8,213 men and suffered 325 killed and 1,277 wounded, a loss rate of 19.5 per cent. Only by the narrowest margins did elements of Sherman's division manage to hold until reinforced by McClernand.

The shock of first contact took a toll on the rebel side as well. Hungry soldiers who passed through the captured Union camps fell out in search of food. Others began looting. Early in the battle, a Mississippi

Union gun teams whip their horses as they retire from an onrushing Confederate assault wave. An officer in the 21st Alabama describes his unit's introduction to combat: 'soon we came in range of the artillery which was thundering like mad in front, the enemy fired too high and the shot crashed among the trees overhead – on! on! we marched – now we could catch glimpse of the [enemy's] white tents through the trees – now the enemy commenced a scattering fire of musketry on us — then the regiment on our right dropped down on their faces and poured a stream of fire upon the enemy – we then got the word and opened on the battery and camp: here fell Herpin and King. Dixon came down a minute later – then we charged into the camp and carried it and the battery; the horses lay dead in their harness all piled up by their own struggles'. (National Archives)

Hard-fighting Brig.Gen. Bushrod Johnson commanded a brigade of Mississippi and Tennessee infantry with characteristic aggression and received a wound during the battle. (US Army Military History Institute)

RIGHT A soldier described the Union retreat to Pittsburg Landing: 'Cavalrymen were riding in all directions with drawn sabres and revolvers threatening to shoot and "Cut men's head off" if they did not stop and rally. Officers were coaxing, praying and exhorting men for "God's sake" to stop and all make a stand together. But in most cases their orders and appeals were not heeded by these demoralised men who kept going like a flock of sheep. All the terrors of hell would not have stopped them until they got to the river.' (Library of Congress)

officer found about 300 stragglers loafing behind his regiment. They told him that they had been badly 'smashed', although in fact they had lost only three or four killed and two dozen wounded. The officer later complained, 'These are the kind of troops of which you read gallant deeds and reckless conduct, they lose half a dozen, retire in time to save their haversacks and are puffed accordingly.'

Back on Prentiss's front, because of Everett Peabody's soldierly conduct, there was time to partially brace the division before the howling line of rebels struck. A defender relates his introduction to combat: 'there was a man just on my right behind a tree and I somewhat envied

SHERMAN'S CAMP IS OVERWHELMED

The 53rd Ohio of Sherman's division were attending to their normal Sunday morning duties unaware of the Confederate steam roller about to engulf them. Together with his staff, Sherman studied through his field glass an unknown force in the distance – it was Hardee's 3rd Corps. Held off for a brief period, eventually the Federal line collapsed and retreated in panic and disorder.

him. He was actively engaged in loading and firing...But, all at once, there he was lying on his back, at the foot of his tree, with one leg doubled under him, motionless, and stone dead!...The event came nearer completely upsetting me than anything else that occurred during the battle – but I got used to such incidents in the course of the day'.

Other units in Prentiss's command experienced the shock of a surprise assault. The 61st Illinois had only been in service for two months and had never seen combat. About 7:30 in the morning a wild-eyed officer rode through camp on a foam-flecked horse. Halting abruptly, knocking over mess tins in the process, he shouted, 'My God! This regiment's not in line yet! They have been fighting on the right for over an hour!' Hastily, the scared men strapped on their equipment and prepared for battle. Whereas the majority of the surprised Federals held their ground, hundreds of others fled to the rear. It was a scene reminiscent of First Bull Run, with soldiers discarding their weapons and running to the rear crying that their unit had been cut to pieces and that they were the only survivors. The shirkers' conduct appalled those who stood firm. They were 'The scum of battles', the 'Dastard bullet dodgers.' When the 11th Iowa moved to the front, one frightened shirker ran by exclaiming, 'Give them hell, boys. I gave them hell as long as I could.' An Iowa soldier recounts: 'Whether he had really given them any, I cannot say, but assuredly he gave them everything else he possessed, including his gun, cartridge box, coat and hat.'

An Illinois soldier describes his inability to prepare himself as the

sounds of musketry approached. Panic 'strikes into the heart of a man [and] it can hardly be conquered. It bewilders and unnerves and maddens'. It also proved infectious. The 15th Iowa was such a green unit that it had received its Springfield muskets only ten days prior to battle. Sunday morning found the regiment eating breakfast aboard a steamer anchored at Pittsburg Landing. Soon orders came to join Prentiss's Division. The regiment marched through hordes of fleeing men until it reached the battle zone. Here it received artillery fire: 'above the roar of the guns could be heard the cheers of our men as they gained ground. At last we could see the enemy and they were advancing around our left flank and the woods seemed alive with gray coats and their victorious cheer and unearthly yells and the concentrated fire which they had upon us caused somebody to give the order for retreat. The word was passed along – and we went off the bloody ground in great confusion'.

The 15th Iowa was not alone. By 9 am, the rebel assault had routed most of Prentiss's division, killed key officers including James Powell and Everett Peabody, and badly battered Sherman's command.

Battle at the tent lines

Where was Grant? As had been the case at Donelson, he was absent from the field during the first hours of the enemy attack. Hearing the sounds of battle, he abandoned his breakfast at his sumptuous headquarters in Savannah and reached the field about 8:30 am. During his steamboat journey to the scene of the fight he passed Crump's Landing where he alerted Lew Wallace's detached division. He also sent word to Brig.Gen. William Nelson (of Buell's army) to hurry to the field. Disembarking at Pittsburg Landing, he organised a straggler line to root out the faint-hearted soldiers who had fled to the shelter of the steep bank along the Tennessee River, and then rode forward to see his lieutenants.

He found Sherman coolly directing his defence on the Union right. Reassured by Sherman's conduct, Grant decided he would leave him pretty much on his own for the balance of the engagement. Grant's troubles rested along his centre and left centre. Whenever heavy enemy pressure forced one of his divisions to retire, it exposed the flanks of the

While this drawing depicts a different action, it clearly shows a Confederate battery wheeling into firing position. 'It was not a good place for a fight,' complained a Louisiana gunner. 'There were very few open and cleared places, the land being hilly and covered densely with trees and undergrowth.' (National Archives)

As Grant steamed towards the battle he paused at Maj.Gen. Lew Wallace's camp to issue Wallace an alert order. Once ordered to march to the fight, Wallace's division took six-and-a-half hours to march 15 miles, failing to arrive until after the first day's fighting ended. (National Archives)

Few of the front-line Union soldiers had time to prepare themselves adequately before they found themselves under fire. By 9 am Brig.Gen. Benjamin Prentiss's two brigades had been driven from the camps. Many of his men ran to the rear, some shouting out to Hurlbut's people, 'You'll catch it! We are cut to pieces. The Rebels are coming!' (National Archives)

adjacent divisions. They in turn would retreat, and this pattern of progressive withdrawals threatened to cause the collapse of the entire line.

However, there was a hidden advantage to the manner in which Grant's divisions had been dispersed in their camps. The Union divisional camps were stacked from Pittsburg Landing outward, and this created a natural series of defensive positions to which they could retire. Inadvertently, the army had a layered defence that amounted to a defence in depth. Secondly, in this war the normal battle response for inexperienced troops and their commanders was to march to the sound of the guns. For the Confederates, this meant packing the front with massed targets and taking losses. For the Federals, it often meant reinforcing a wavering line just when it needed help. Thus, the battle featured Confederate assaults against a succession of backstopping positions, and this process wore down their strength.

The defenders, sheltered in the woods along the borders of the fields, were well hidden. The attackers, who had to advance across the open fields, provided good targets. Three rebels' accounts underscore this phenomenon. A Texas captain recalls crossing a field and wondering 'where is the enemy?' Suddenly, 'the fence before us became trans-

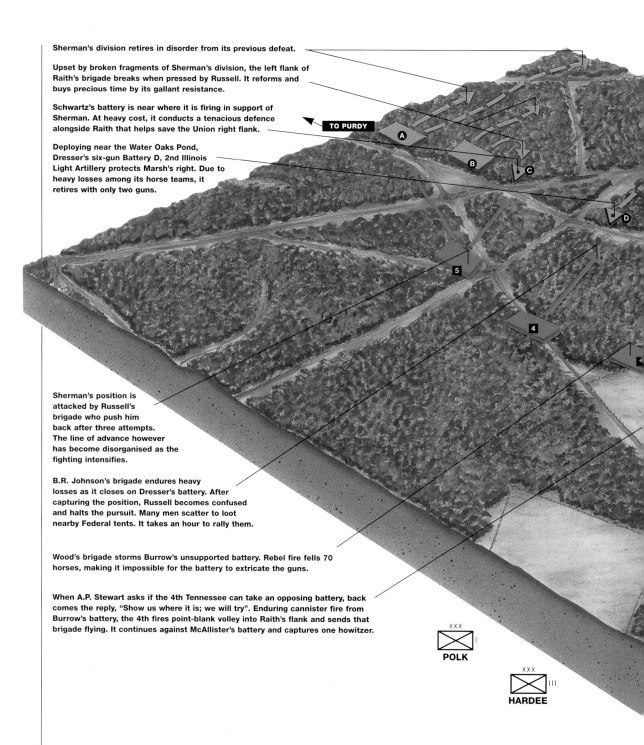

Sherman's division retires in disorder from its previous defeat.

Upset by broken fragments of Sherman's division, the left flank of Raith's brigade breaks when pressed by Russell. It reforms and buys precious time by its gallant resistance.

Schwartz's battery is near where it is firing in support of Sherman. At heavy cost, it conducts a tenacious defence alongside Raith that helps save the Union right flank.

TO PURDY

Deploying near the Water Oaks Pond, Dresser's six-gun Battery D, 2nd Illinois Light Artillery protects Marsh's right. Due to heavy losses among its horse teams, it retires with only two guns.

Sherman's position is attacked by Russell's brigade who push him back after three attempts. The line of advance however has become disorganised as the fighting intensifies.

B.R. Johnson's brigade endures heavy losses as it closes on Dresser's battery. After capturing the position, Russell becomes confused and halts the pursuit. Many men scatter to loot nearby Federal tents. It takes an hour to rally them.

Wood's brigade storms Burrow's unsupported battery. Rebel fire fells 70 horses, making it impossible for the battery to extricate the guns.

When A.P. Stewart asks if the 4th Tennessee can take an opposing battery, back comes the reply, "Show us where it is; we will try". Enduring cannister fire from Burrow's battery, the 4th fires point-blank volley into Raith's flank and sends that brigade flying. It continues against McAllister's battery and captures one howitzer.

XXX
POLK

XXX
HARDEE

BATTLE OF SHILOH 1862, THE CONFEDERATE ATTACK

6 April 1030 - 1200 hours, viewed from the south-east. Following the initial skirmishing in the early hours of the morning, the Confederates launched their full-scale attack on the Union right where Sherman and McClernand's troops were camped.

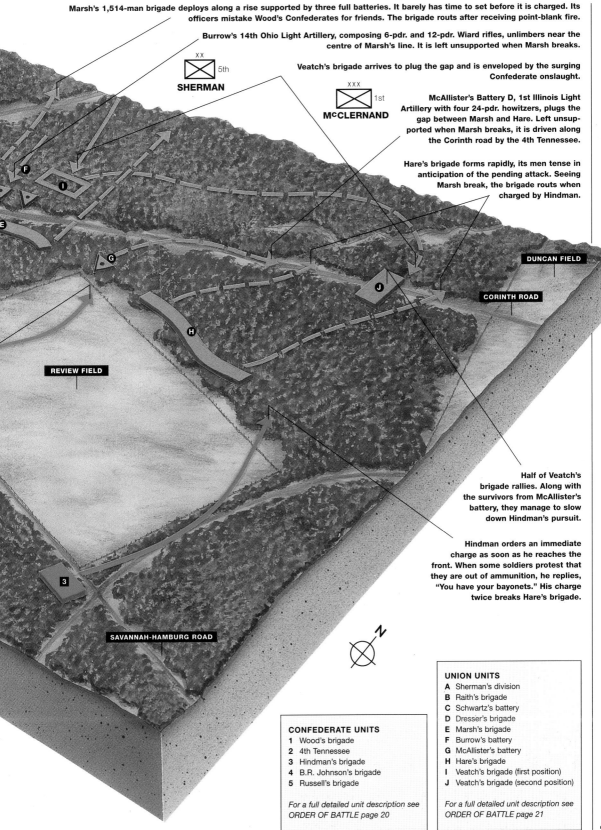

Marsh's 1,514-man brigade deploys along a rise supported by three full batteries. It barely has time to set before it is charged. Its officers mistake Wood's Confederates for friends. The brigade routs after receiving point-blank fire.

Burrow's 14th Ohio Light Artillery, composing 6-pdr. and 12-pdr. Wiard rifles, unlimbers near the centre of Marsh's line. It is left unsupported when Marsh breaks.

Veatch's brigade arrives to plug the gap and is enveloped by the surging Confederate onslaught.

McAllister's Battery D, 1st Illinois Light Artillery with four 24-pdr. howitzers, plugs the gap between Marsh and Hare. Left unsupported when Marsh breaks, it is driven along the Corinth road by the 4th Tennessee.

Hare's brigade forms rapidly, its men tense in anticipation of the pending attack. Seeing Marsh break, the brigade routs when charged by Hindman.

XX 5th
SHERMAN

XXX 1st
McCLERNAND

DUNCAN FIELD

CORINTH ROAD

REVIEW FIELD

Half of Veatch's brigade rallies. Along with the survivors from McAllister's battery, they manage to slow down Hindman's pursuit.

Hindman orders an immediate charge as soon as he reaches the front. When some soldiers protest that they are out of ammunition, he replies, "You have your bayonets." His charge twice breaks Hare's brigade.

SAVANNAH-HAMBURG ROAD

N

CONFEDERATE UNITS
1 Wood's brigade
2 4th Tennessee
3 Hindman's brigade
4 B.R. Johnson's brigade
5 Russell's brigade

For a full detailed unit description see ORDER OF BATTLE page 20

UNION UNITS
A Sherman's division
B Raith's brigade
C Schwartz's battery
D Dresser's brigade
E Marsh's brigade
F Burrow's battery
G McAllister's battery
H Hare's brigade
I Veatch's brigade (first position)
J Veatch's brigade (second position)

For a full detailed unit description see ORDER OF BATTLE page 21

43

formed into a wall of flame'. All an Arkansas soldier saw of the enemy was 'a blurry line of figures dressed in blue as volley after volley was exchanged'. This was more than a soldier in the 6th Mississippi saw. Charging at the run he saw no-one, even though the enemy bullets began striking hard and fast. All he and his comrades perceived were 'little clouds of smoke'.

In contrast, the defenders frequently had a fine view of their enemy's advance. A Michigan infantryman could plainly observe how 'their lines begin to unfold and develop'. However, once the attackers halted to return fire, dense clouds of smoke concealed the rival lines. An Illinois private who was an experienced hunter accustomed to husbanding his ammunition until a good shot presented itself, found hunting rebels very different from hunting game: 'the Confederates halted and began firing also, and the fronts of both lines were at once shrouded in smoke. I had my gun at the ready, and was trying to peer under the smoke in order to get a sight of our enemies. Suddenly I heard some one in a highly excited tone calling to me just in my rear, – "Stillwell! shoot! shoot! Why don't you shoot?"'

Obeying his lieutenant, Stillwell blazed away through the smoke, all the while doubting he could possibly hit anything. The volume of unaimed fire astonished him. The return fire passing overhead sounded like a swarm of bees.

Fighting in the woods themselves was even more confused. Soldiers on both sides dispersed behind all available cover. It became a deadly game of hide-and-seek among the trees. An Illinois soldier told his wife that 'the hardes [sic] thing to do was to get a sight of a rebel before they

Arriving on the battlefield, Grant looked disaster square in the face and refused to panic. (Library of Congress)

A political appointee, Maj.Gen. John McClernand displayed courage and little else. His division's piecemeal commitment caused heavy losses. (Library of Congress)

Colonel William Bate commanded the 2nd Tennessee. During the attack on Sherman's camps, Bate spied a Federal battery and led his regiment 'briskly to the charge'. A Minie ball broke his leg forcing him to be carried from the field. Inexperienced at war, Bate had failed to inform his second-in-command of his intention to charge. This officer, who was on the regiment's opposite flank when Bate was hit, halted the regiment in mid-charge. Wounded on two other fields, Bate was offered the governorship of Tennessee in 1863. He declined, saying that as long as the Yankees were in his state, his duty was to fight, not to reap civil honours. (Tennessee State Library and Archives)

While the 4th Tennessee was lying down under a hail of grape and shell some 800 yards from a Federal battery, word came from Bragg that this battery must be taken. The regiment's colonel replied that he would try. He advanced the regiment, cleverly avoiding the open field where previous assaults had failed. He marched it at the double through a dense thicket until it came to within 30 yards of the battery. The 4th Tennessee fired one volley, cheered, and charged to overrun the battery. Even though the regiment had manoeuvred carefully, taking advantage of terrain and approaching the battery from the side, it still suffered badly, losing 31 men killed and another 130 wounded, most of them during this charge. The battery in this photo fell to a charge boring in from the thicket to the gun's left. (Author's collection)

move...It seemed to me that they were all deers but they was a good deal worse for while I was looking for them they were firing at me'.

Amid the confusion two themes began to emerge: in spite of the shock, enough of Grant's men were still going to fight and to fight hard; in spite of his surprise, Grant was maintaining his balance. However, the lack of cohesion among his divisions threatened to undo these efforts.

This was clear during McClernand's Division's fight, which was characterised by confusion and disorder. Men and officers alike had heard the surprising and unsettling sound of firing from Sherman's and Prentiss's camps. Slowly they comprehended that a battle had begun. The division advanced piecemeal into the void between Sherman and Prentiss and never was able to align solidly. A lack of tactical direction from superior officers meant that each regiment believed it fought in isolation. Many had no time to brace themselves before they found themselves under fire from what seemed to be an overwhelming mass of rebels, and some broke at first contact. Others fought until they perceived that the adjacent units had retired and thus exposed their flanks.

The consequences of piecemeal commitment are illustrated by the experiences of Col. Julius Raith's Brigade. Acting independently, at 8 am Raith marched toward the sounds of firing to support Sherman. His men had to shoulder through a horde of retreating soldiers before deploying. Raith saw elements of three rebel brigades approaching. Realising that he had no support on his left, he tried to revitalise that flank, but before he could do it, the Confederate assault crumbled his flank. Just then a staff officer rode up to order the brigade to withdraw in order to link up with

a second, newly arrived Union brigade. The orders tumbled out to the men in short succession: 'fire to front', 'face flank', 'retreat'. It was too much. Soon Raith's Brigade was running to the rear.

The experience of McClernand's Second Brigade, commanded by Col. Carroll Marsh, were similar. The brigade barely had time to deploy before its soldiers saw a large force steadily advancing toward them. Because of mistaken identity, they held fire until the attackers were 30 yards away. A few infantrymen fired only to hear one of their officers shout 'Cease fire! Those are our troops'. 'The hell they are!' replied a private and then proof came when the rebels fired and charged. 'Our men fell like autumn leaves,' recalls a survivor. 'During the first five minutes,' wrote Marsh, 'I lost more in killed and wounded than in all the other actions.' In spite of the fact they were Donelson veterans, poor leadership undid the brigade and it retreated.

The manner in which one breach could cause an entire line to unravel now became apparent. Marsh's débâcle left McAllister's Battery unsupported. The battery's four 24-pdr. howitzers had been dominating

CASUALTIES FROM 'FRIENDLY FIRE'

Like so much of the fighting in the Civil War, Shiloh featured close range combat in wooded terrain. Opponents could barely see one another. Units fired at the flashes from enemy muskets. The appearance of a shadowy enemy battle line on flank or rear spelled doom.

the ground and stalling the Confederate advance. General Braxton Bragg ordered Brig.Gen. Alexander Stewart to storm the position. Stewart rode to the colonel of the 4th Tennessee and asked if his regiment could do the job. 'We will try', the colonel replied. The 4th Tennessee double-quicked through a thicket to outflank the battery, a move that was possible because of the absence of the battery's infantry supports. When 30 paces from the guns, the regiment halted, delivered a volley, and rushed forward with a yell. McAllister, wounded in four places, gave the order to limber and retire. Horse losses had been so heavy that he had to leave one gun behind. However, the battery's grape and canister fire killed 31 and wounded about 160 men of the 4th Tennessee.

In turn, Col. Abraham Hare's Federal brigade witnessed the rebel assault bear down against Marsh's Brigade and McAllister's Battery and overrun their position. 'Seeing the enemy approaching in great

Grant immediately ordered his cavalry to round up stragglers and return them to the front. A fine study of the carbine-carrying 5th Ohio Cavalry taken two months after Shiloh. During the battle the regiment performed provost duty. (Library of Congress)

Brigadier-General Thomas Hindman was one of the many Confederate officers present at Shiloh who developed into aggressive, capable combat leaders. His brigade helped smash Sherman's line and overrun McClernand's artillery. (Tennessee State Library and Archives)

numbers,' relates Hare, 'and our troops on the right having given way, my regiments also broke and retired in confusion'. Although Hare managed to rally them, all that remained of McClernand's first battle line was unsupported artillery. Burrows' 14th Ohio Battery occupied a position behind Marsh's line. After McAllister retired, two regiments of Wood's Brigade worked their way forward. The ferocious Confederate close-range fire dropped 70 horses, rendering the battery immobile, and Wood's men captured it intact.

Next came Dresser's Battery D, 2nd Illinois Light Artillery. Although the battery retained the support of the 11th Iowa, it had to face determined assaults from the 154th Tennessee and Blythe's Mississippi regiment. Sherman's chief of artillery, a veteran of two battles, praised the battery's defence and said the fighting here was 'the most terrific' of the entire day. An Iowa soldier praised the rebel assault: 'Without a waver the long line of glittering steel moved steadily forward.' A brief, tremendous struggle ensued, but the attackers shrugged off their losses and reached the guns. Panicked battery horses dashed to the rear, scattering the supporting Union infantry. The 11th Iowa's colonel was unhorsed, its major shot in the head. The Federal position collapsed and the attackers captured another four guns. The Confederate assault had broken McClernand's line and nearly destroyed all of his artillery.

Confederate Brig.Gen. Thomas Hindman pressed forward with as many men as he could find. When some infantry protested that they were out of ammunition, Hindman replied, 'You have your bayonets.' Again Hare's Brigade broke (once more complaining that the adjacent units broke first). But the attackers had paid a terrible price and now they confronted 3,000 fresh enemy troops belonging to Col. James Veatch's Brigade from Hurlbut's Division. As had been the case with the succession of Union brigades, Veatch's men fought without supports to

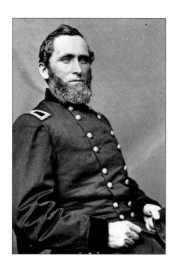

Brigadier-General Benjamin Prentiss managed to rally some of his division to hold the centre of the Hornets' Nest. (Library of Congress)

BELOW **From the woods in the background Confederate troops emerged to attack the Union line behind this fence line at the Hornets' Nest. The Hornets' Nest was easily the best defensive position along any part of Grant's line, largely because of its open fields of fire. (Author's collection)**

either flank. 'Everything was confusion around us, a perfect storm of shell and bullets,' relates an Illinois captain. Suffering serious officer losses, Veatch's regiments lost tactical order. The 46th Illinois tried to dress ranks after being disrupted by retreating troops, only to suffer an enfilade fire from the right that hit nearly half of the men on that flank, including another eight officers. Half of Veatch's Brigade routed, but the balance, supported by McAllister's three remaining 24-pdrs., managed to disrupt Hindman's pursuit.

Contributing to the slowdown of the Confederate assault was the performance of the rebel high command. Hardee, who had been in charge here, was satisfied that Hindman was performing well and departed to see how matters stood on his right. Here was another pernicious effect of the long Confederate battle line. The senior commanders had to move along an overly extensive front to try to control the advance. Shortly after Hardee departed Hindman went down with a wound. This left a command void made worse by the fact that when Bragg arrived with his second wave, he concluded that the rebels on this sector were fought out and so he also moved off to the right. Eventually Hardee, Bragg, and Polk made an informal agreement to divide the front, with Polk given command of the left. By the time the bishop-warrior appeared he found his troops too scattered and depleted to press on.

Even though they had been poorly served by their superior officers, Sherman's and McClernand's men had managed to slow the Confederate onslaught against the Union right. At noon the rallied Federal soldiers would even manage to mount a 45-minute long counterattack. Another indication of the spirit of McClernand's division was the fact that there were only 85 men missing out of their 1,742 casualties. As the fighting on the Union right ebbed, the battle hinged on what became known as the 'Hornets' Nest', a sunken farm lane blocking a direct Confederate thrust to Pittsburg Landing.

The Hornets' Nest

By 9 am the Confederate assault had breached the Union centre, and the majority of Prentiss's men were retreating toward Pittsburg Landing. Fortunately for the Federal cause, Brig.Gen. Stephen Hurlbut appeared with two fresh brigades to fill the hole. Because their divisional camps were well back from the front line, Hurlbut's soldiers had not been caught up in the initial surprise assault. They had time to form in line of battle and await orders. At 7:30 am a request had come from Sherman for help. Hurlbut immediately sent one brigade to

**Impatient with the lack of
progress against the Hornets'
Nest, Gen. Braxton Bragg rode
up to a regiment that had twice
failed in an assault. When its
wounded colonel protested that
the position could not be conquered frontally, Bragg shamed
him by retorting, 'Serve them as
they have served you' and sent
them in on a third charge.**

bolster the Union right. Thirty minutes later Prentiss asked for reinforcements, too. Hurlbut marched his remaining two brigades, about
4,500 men, along with his artillery and cavalry down the Hamburg-
Savannah road toward the sounds of firing.

They quickly encountered the broken debris of Prentiss's command.
The panic-stricken soldiers, shouting 'We're whipped, we're whipped;
we're all cut to pieces!', blocked the road. It was a dangerous moment.
But most of Hurlbut's men had beaten the rebels once before at Fort
Donelson and the contagion of fear did not spread to them. Contemp-
tuously shouldering their way through Prentiss's 'panic-stricken
wretches' they pressed on to occupy a defensive position about a half-
mile behind Prentiss's camps. The V-shaped position was like a
breakwater pointing toward the surging Confederate line. Rebel
gunners quickly found them. One of their first rounds killed the horse
of Col. Williams who led Hurlbut's First Brigade. Another blew up an
ammunition caisson of Meyer's Ohio Battery, frightened the horses, and

The farm track, often called the 'sunken lane', at the centre of the Hornets' Nest. (Author's collection)

sent the inexperienced crew running rearward in panic. But the combat veterans ignored all of this and instead concentrated on the advancing grey infantry who suddenly appeared across the field.

Had the Confederate advance been well managed, there would have been sufficient men to overwhelm Hurlbut. However, reports of a Union division marching against his army's right, forced Sidney Johnston to re-direct two brigades poised to attack Hurlbut against the imagined threat. Furthermore, Wood's and Shaver's brigades had turned west to attack toward Sherman. This left only Adams's hard-used brigade to confront Hurlbut's two brigades. The bluecoats believed that they faced a significant assault. In fact, it was a mere two-company reconnaissance force that was easily repulsed. Around 9:30 am Johnston ordered his Reserve Corps to come up, but it was more than two hours distant. A desultory artillery duel ensued and during this time many of Prentiss's men rallied and joined Hurlbut's line. Additionally, most of W.H.L. Wallace's division also came up. Henceforth, it would take a major effort to break this new Federal position. The Confederates had wasted a grand opportunity.

Indeed, on the Confederate side, grand tactical manoeuvre had quickly become impossible because the reserves had been committed too early. Polk's Corps, constituting the third 'wave' of the rebel surge, had barely moved forward when Johnston ordered one of its brigades to enter the battle on the right. Shortly after, Beauregard ordered another of Polk's brigades to support the left. Inevitably, further orders soon arrived for the remaining two brigades to enter the fray in the middle.

Regiments belonging to Maj.Gen. Benjamin Cheatham's division made some of the first charges against the Hornets' Nest. Cheatham, who reported that they were driven back by a 'murderous crossfire', was wounded during the battle. (Tennessee State Library and Archives)

Along the 'sunken lane', canister-firing Union artillery fired point blank at charging rebels. (Library of Congress)

So, with the battle still in its early stages, four-sevenths of the reserves had been committed.

Throughout the day the Federal artillery served as the lynchpins of the defence. As long as a battery had enough ammunition and infantry supports to protect its flanks, it could control its front with lethal blasts of canister. Retreating, friendly infantry who still had fight in them naturally converged around a friendly battery to form strong resistance centres. Beauregard's imperative to march toward the sound of the heaviest firing meant that too often rebel reserves used themselves up attacking the most formidable defences, the Union artillery positions. Naked bayonet charges could overcome this resistance, but only at a terrible price.

Also contributing to the impulse to march toward the enemy artillery was the unsophisticated tactical direction provided by Confederate staff officer Col. Jordan. Jordan had been present at the first battle of Bull Run, and on that field his duties required him to remain in the rear. At Shiloh he reminded Beauregard of this fact and asked to be allowed to go forward. Beauregard kindly assented, but it proved a lethal mistake. Like many staff officers, Jordan fancied himself a tactician. As he rode toward the firing he passed unengaged lines of men. He noticed that the division and corps commanders seemed absent, a fact caused by the unwise linear dispersion inherent in Beauregard's deployment for battle. Taking an untoward liberty, in the name of Gen. Johnston, Jordan ordered the reserves to enter the battle by heading towards the sound of the heaviest firing. Worse, he encountered the chiefs of staff of three of the four rebel corps, as well as Johnston's chief aide-de-camp, and repeated his tactical insight to them all. Soon these officers were coursing the field to send every available man into combat. The result was that additional rebel forces marched toward the locations where

determined Confederate assaults had already been repulsed by loud, canister-firing Union batteries. A bloodbath ensued.

Largely by chance, elements of three Union divisions – W.H.L. Wallace, Prentiss, and Hurlbut – held Grant's centre. In the middle stood perhaps 1,000 of Prentiss's men who occupied a worn farm track. This 'sunken road', in fact merely a shallow depression at the time of the battle, served as a natural rallying point. Its strength lay in the clear line of sight presented by the open field in front. To Prentiss's left were Hurlbut's two brigades. Lauman's Brigade occupied an extension of the farm path, while Isaac Pugh deployed his brigade in front of a peach orchard that overlooked an old cotton field. W.H.L. Wallace, with 5,800 men, held a strong position in woods bordering the Duncan Field. As the afternoon passed, about 11,000 Union men, supported by seven batteries numbering 38 guns, engaged along this half-mile-long line. At least 18,000 Confederates assaulted them, yet they failed to mass even 4,000 men in any one attack.

Units belonging to Confederate Maj.Gen. Ben Cheatham's Division participated in one of the early charges. They had to cross 300 yards of open ground before reaching the opposing line. The soldiers double-quicked through an artillery barrage across the Duncan Field. Here they encountered the 14th Iowa, whose colonel had skilfully deployed his regiment on the reverse slope of a small ridge. Ordered to lie down, the Iowa soldiers waited until the attackers came within 30 paces. Then the regiment fired. They 'completely destroyed' the first rebel line. Adjacent Federal units joined in to deliver what Cheatham called a 'murderous cross-fire'. Having left the ground 'literally covered' with fallen men, Cheatham's survivors retreated.

Soon thereafter Confederate Gen. Braxton Bragg took tactical charge of the combat. Without any reconnaissance, Bragg ordered Col. Randall Gibson's four-regiment brigade to advance. Gibson's men marched through a dense thicket toward Prentiss's sunken road position. They never saw what hit them. Suddenly a shower of musketry swept their ranks. Two 6-pdr. brass guns fired canister from a knoll behind Prentiss's line, while Lauman's and Wallace's men joined in from the flank. One of Gibson's colonels reported that it was 'a perfect rain of bullets, shot and shell'. So shocked and confused were the attackers that an Arkansas colonel believed the fire was mistakenly coming from friendly troops. The attackers could not endure it and fell back in disorder. Bragg believed their conduct was disgraceful and sent an officer to rally them.

A lull ensued during which Grant arrived behind Prentiss's line. He studied the situation and realised that Prentiss held the key to his army's fate. Telling Prentiss that Lew Wallace would soon arrive to reinforce his position, Grant ordered him to 'maintain that position at all hazards'.

Meanwhile, overriding the protests of Gibson and his officers, Bragg ordered another charge. This time Gibson's Brigade advanced through the canister fire until it came to within 20 yards of the sunken road. Suddenly the defenders rose and fired. A rebel private related that the defenders 'mow[ed] us down at every volley', until so many men were shot that it looked like a 'slaughter pen'. Receiving fire from three directions, the attackers charged up to the very muzzles of the Union artillery where a brief hand-to-hand fight took place. But Gibson's gallant men were unsupported and they could not long endure the

RIGHT **At this time, on the Union left, McArthur and Stuart find their left flanks enveloped and retreat to Pittsburg Landing. Due to the lack of reserves and Johnston's mortal wound, suffered around 2:30 pm, the Confederates fail to advance behind Grant's army toward the Landing. Instead, all attention focuses on breaching the Hornet's Nest in a series of assaults that last from 3 to 5:30 pm.**

CONFEDERATE OPPORTUNITY, 3 PM, 6 APRIL 1862

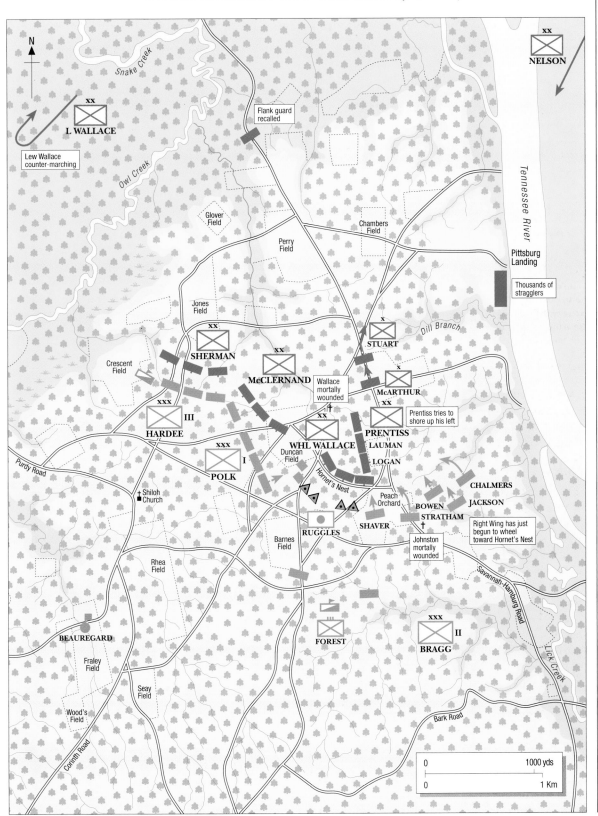

N

NELSON
xx

Snake Creek

L WALLACE
xx

Lew Wallace
counter-marching

Owl Creek

Flank guard
recalled

Tennessee River

Glover
Field

Perry
Field

Chambers
Field

Pittsburg
Landing

Jones
Field

Thousands of
stragglers

Crescent
Field

SHERMAN
xx

McCLERNAND
xx

STUART
x

Dill Branch

Wallace
mortally
wounded

McARTHUR
x

HARDEE
xxx
III

WHL WALLACE
xx

PRENTISS
xx

Prentiss tries to
shore up his left

Purdy Road

POLK
xxx
I

Duncan
Field

LAUMAN

LOGAN

Shiloh
Church

Hornet's Nest

Peach
Orchard

CHALMERS

JACKSON

RUGGLES

SHAVER

BOWEN

STRATHAM

Right Wing has just
begun to wheel
toward Hornet's Nest

Barnes
Field

Johnston
mortally
wounded

Rhea
Field

Savannah-Hamburg Road

FOREST
xxx

BRAGG
xxx
II

BEAUREGARD

Fraley
Field

Lick Creek

Seay
Field

Wood's
Field

Bark Road

Corinth Road

| 0 | | 1000 yds |
| 0 | | 1 Km |

Colonel William Preston, Sidney Johnston's former brother-in-law, found the general still breathing some ten minutes after being wounded. 'Johnston, do you know me?' he cried. Receiving no response, Preston searched for a body wound, failing to find the actual death wound that had cut a large artery behind Johnston's knee. Fifteen minutes later Johnston was dead. (National Archives)

Brigadier-General Stephen Hurlbut plugged the hole in the Union centre. His arrival at the front with two fresh brigades allowed the Federal troops to form a cohesive defensive position at the Hornets' Nest. (Library of Congress)

uneven contest. When the smoke cleared, the defenders saw their foe in torn and mangled heaps. The brush through which the attackers had passed had been chopped low by canister fire and looked like a corn field after harvest. One of Gibson's survivors said the stinging Federal fire was like facing a swarm of hornets. Thus the Union position became known as the 'Hornets' Nest'.

Gibson's second repulse displeased Bragg. He would later write that Gibson's men were driven back merely by a skirmish line of sharp-shooters. His comment underscores an incredible ignorance of battlefield reality. Bragg ordered Gibson to attack again. When one of Gibson's colonels, who was dripping blood from a face wound, protested that the position could not be conquered frontally and instead had to be attacked in flank, Bragg shamed him by retorting, 'Col. Allen, I want no faltering now'. So the brigade attacked a third time, briefly managed to come close to the Federal line, and failed once more.

Next it was the turn of Shaver's Brigade. It had failed once already against this position, retired to refit and re-supply, and returned. At Bragg's order it advanced around 2 pm and attacked against a different sector where the undergrowth was so thick that Shaver could not see a Union battery until it opened a lethal, close-range fire. Shaver reported, 'I pressed forward [to within 60 yards] when a terrific and murderous fire was poured in upon me from their lines and battery. It was impossible to charge through the dense undergrowth, and I soon discovered my fire was having no effect upon the enemy, so I had nothing left me but to retire or have my men all shot down'.

As more Confederate units arrived, including Breckinridge's reserves, they would conduct additional bloody assaults. At least ten, and perhaps 12 charges took place here. In the end, as Col. Allen had explained to Bragg, it would indeed be flank pressure that gained the position.

Death of a general

Sidney Johnston's plan had been to concentrate against the Union left flank in order to drive Grant's men away from Pittsburg Landing. However, the clumsy initial Confederate deployment failed to bring battle to this flank until four hours after the opening assault against Prentiss and Sherman. Perturbed, around 11 am Johnston rode toward his right flank. Joining him were two of Breckinridge's brigades. In total there were some 8,000 infantry confronting a mere two Federal brigades. The ground adjacent to the Tennessee River was the most rugged terrain on the field: a series of deep ravines topped by wooded ridges ran perpendicular to the river. Behind one of these ravines, Stuart's Brigade of Union troops grappled with one-and-a-half Confederate brigades for two hours. Meanwhile, McArthur's three-regiment brigade held the more important position between the Peach Orchard and Stuart (to the Union left of the Hornets' Nest). Against it came seven Confederate regiments.

The rebels' inexperience coupled with the difficult terrain meant that the attack proceeded cautiously. A time-consuming, long-range fire fight took place. The difficulty of urging his men forward frustrated Gen. Breckinridge. He rode to Johnston's entourage and claimed that he could not get one of his brigades to charge. Along with his volunteer aide-de-camp, Tennessee Governor Isham Harris, Johnston rode to the front to lead the men forward. The soldiers belonged to Statham's Brigade and at this point, shortly before 2 pm, they had the Confederacy's highest ranking field general, the former vice-president of the United States, and the Confederate governor of Tennessee to lead them. Inspired, the brigade rose up, cheered wildly, and joined by Bowen's and Jackson's brigades, charged toward the Peach Orchard.

The defenders of the Peach Orchard had been fighting for nearly six hours. They had suffered serious losses and were short of ammunition. As the attacking line swept towards them they saw that McArthur's small brigade holding their left was breaking apart. Mann's Battery turned to face the flank and delivered punishing canister fire. It was not enough. A half-mile gap opened up between the Peach Orchard and Stuart's Brigade and into this void poured thousands of grey-clad infantry. The sight unnerved some of the men defending the Peach Orchard, and when Statham's Brigade pressed through the defender's artillery fire and drew near, the 41st Illinois broke and ran. In the absence of infantry supports, the artillery had to try to withdraw as well.

Out in the open, in front of the Peach Orchard, Sidney Johnston sat astride Fire-eater and watched the battle being won. Elated, he hardly noticed that he had received a wound. A Minie ball had torn an artery behind his right knee. It was a serious wound but would not have been fatal if the blood flow was stanched. Johnston had a field tourniquet in his pocket that would have done the job. Instead, unmindful of his injury, he continued to direct the attack until he slumped in his saddle and turned pale. His aides took him to the rear and sought ineffectually to assist him. Shortly afterwards Sidney Johnston died of blood loss.

About this time, Col. Jordan arrived nearby. Although few reserves remained, Jordan managed to find one brigade belonging to Breckinridge's Reserve Corps. Glancing at his timepiece, Jordan saw that it was 2:20 pm. By Jordan's understanding the battle should have been won by now. Accordingly, he decided that the reserves should be committed, and ordered the reserve brigade into the fray in Johnston's name. Jordan

Brigadier-General Daniel Ruggles, one of the few Confederate officers to appreciate that artillery firepower could be used in place of naked valour, formed a massed battery to bombard the Hornets' Nest. (Library of Congress)

A Blakely rifle on Ruggles' gun line. The Union line was 500 yards across the clearing, in the wood line in the background. (Author's collection)

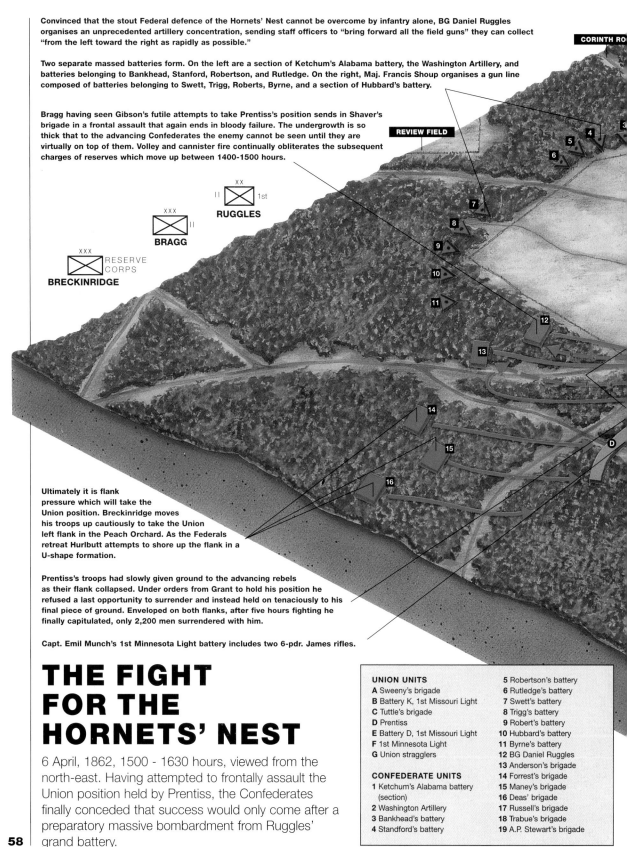

Convinced that the stout Federal defence of the Hornets' Nest cannot be overcome by infantry alone, BG Daniel Ruggles organises an unprecedented artillery concentration, sending staff officers to "bring forward all the field guns" they can collect "from the left toward the right as rapidly as possible."

Two separate massed batteries form. On the left are a section of Ketchum's Alabama battery, the Washington Artillery, and batteries belonging to Bankhead, Stanford, Robertson, and Rutledge. On the right, Maj. Francis Shoup organises a gun line composed of batteries belonging to Swett, Trigg, Roberts, Byrne, and a section of Hubbard's battery.

Bragg having seen Gibson's futile attempts to take Prentiss's position sends in Shaver's brigade in a frontal assault that again ends in bloody failure. The undergrowth is so thick that to the advancing Confederates the enemy cannot be seen until they are virtually on top of them. Volley and cannister fire continually obliterates the subsequent charges of reserves which move up between 1400-1500 hours.

CORINTH RO

REVIEW FIELD

RUGGLES

BRAGG

BRECKINRIDGE — RESERVE CORPS

Ultimately it is flank pressure which will take the Union position. Breckinridge moves his troops up cautiously to take the Union left flank in the Peach Orchard. As the Federals retreat Hurlbutt attempts to shore up the flank in a U-shape formation.

Prentiss's troops had slowly given ground to the advancing rebels as their flank collapsed. Under orders from Grant to hold his position he refused a last opportunity to surrender and instead held on tenaciously to his final piece of ground. Enveloped on both flanks, after five hours fighting he finally capitulated, only 2,200 men surrendered with him.

Capt. Emil Munch's 1st Minnesota Light battery includes two 6-pdr. James rifles.

THE FIGHT FOR THE HORNETS' NEST

6 April, 1862, 1500 - 1630 hours, viewed from the north-east. Having attempted to frontally assault the Union position held by Prentiss, the Confederates finally conceded that success would only come after a preparatory massive bombardment from Ruggles' grand battery.

UNION UNITS	
A Sweeny's brigade	**5** Robertson's battery
B Battery K, 1st Missouri Light	**6** Rutledge's battery
C Tuttle's brigade	**7** Swett's battery
D Prentiss	**8** Trigg's battery
E Battery D, 1st Missouri Light	**9** Robert's battery
F 1st Minnesota Light	**10** Hubbard's battery
G Union stragglers	**11** Byrne's battery
	12 BG Daniel Ruggles
CONFEDERATE UNITS	**13** Anderson's brigade
1 Ketchum's Alabama battery (section)	**14** Forrest's brigade
	15 Maney's brigade
2 Washington Artillery	**16** Deas' brigade
3 Bankhead's battery	**17** Russell's brigade
4 Standford's battery	**18** Trabue's brigade
	19 A.P. Stewart's brigade

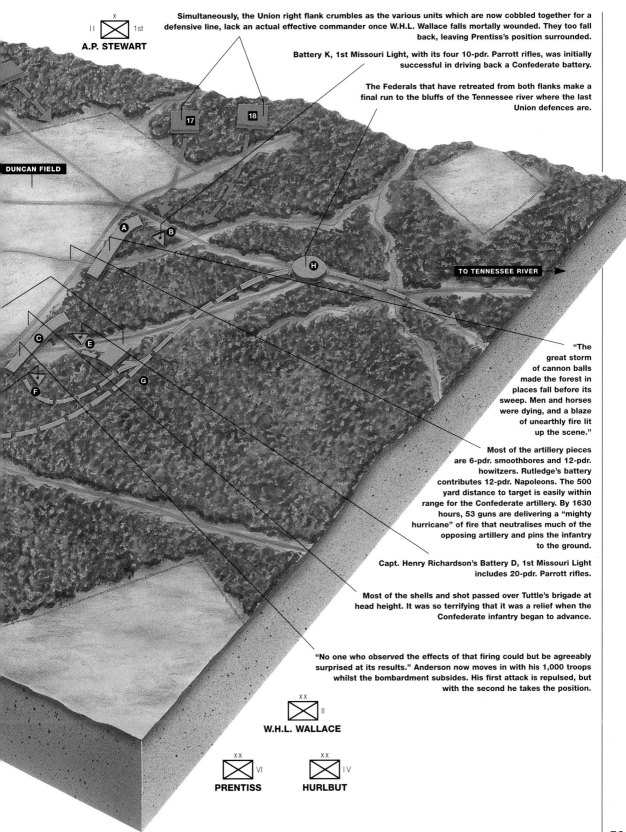

A.P. STEWART

II ☒ 1st
X

Simultaneously, the Union right flank crumbles as the various units which are now cobbled together for a defensive line, lack an actual effective commander once W.H.L. Wallace falls mortally wounded. They too fall back, leaving Prentiss's position surrounded.

Battery K, 1st Missouri Light, with its four 10-pdr. Parrott rifles, was initially successful in driving back a Confederate battery.

The Federals that have retreated from both flanks make a final run to the bluffs of the Tennessee river where the last Union defences are.

DUNCAN FIELD

17

18

A

B

H

TO TENNESSEE RIVER →

C

E

G

F

"The great storm of cannon balls made the forest in places fall before its sweep. Men and horses were dying, and a blaze of unearthly fire lit up the scene."

Most of the artillery pieces are 6-pdr. smoothbores and 12-pdr. howitzers. Rutledge's battery contributes 12-pdr. Napoleons. The 500 yard distance to target is easily within range for the Confederate artillery. By 1630 hours, 53 guns are delivering a "mighty hurricane" of fire that neutralises much of the opposing artillery and pins the infantry to the ground.

Capt. Henry Richardson's Battery D, 1st Missouri Light includes 20-pdr. Parrott rifles.

Most of the shells and shot passed over Tuttle's brigade at head height. It was so terrifying that it was a relief when the Confederate infantry began to advance.

"No one who observed the effects of that firing could but be agreeably surprised at its results." Anderson now moves in with his 1,000 troops whilst the bombardment subsides. His first attack is repulsed, but with the second he takes the position.

XX
☒ II
W.H.L. WALLACE

XX
☒ VI
PRENTISS

XX
☒ IV
HURLBUT

The 32nd Illinois defends the Peach Orchard. A rebel battle line reforms across the field. The area in the left background is where Johnston was hit. (Library of Congress)

Colonel John Logan commanded the 32nd Illinois. Hurlbut rushed Logan to his embattled left flank when the Confederate advance began to turn his flank at the Peach Orchard. (National Archives)

did not know that Johnston was recently dead, nor did he know that a carefully husbanded reserve could have capitalised on yet another fine opportunity.

At the time of Johnston's death, his infantry had carved a breach in the Federal line from the Peach Orchard to the Tennessee River. No organised Union force stood between the victorious infantry and Pittsburg Landing a mile-and-a-half distant. But in Johnston's absence, Breckinridge – the ranking officer here – failed to press the advantage. Recall that Johnston's battle plan called for a rupture of the Union left and then a drive to pin Grant's army against Owl Creek. In addition, the rebel leaders had heard the din of battle in front of the Hornets' Nest, and realised that they were now in position to envelope the Union line. Accordingly, four Confederate brigades began a left wheel away from Pittsburg Landing toward the exposed Federal flank.

At the same time, renewed pressure came directly on the defenders near the Peach Orchard. Here, waiting Union soldiers watched the Confederates mass for the attack. The assault waves 'leaped the fence, line after line, and formed on the opposite side of the field', recalled an Iowa soldier, and then came on, 'dressing their ranks, hedges of bayonets gleaming above them, and their proud banners waving in the breeze'. The defenders' fire soon reduced this martial display to scores of dead men who 'lay so thickly upon the field...that they looked like a line of troops lying down to receive our fire'. Although the defenders continued to repulse frontal attacks, the movement of three brigades – Bowen, Jackson, and Chalmers – overlapped Prentiss's left flank. The Federals ceded the Peach Orchard and retired into a U-shaped perimeter. General Hurlbut cobbled together a makeshift line to defend Prentiss's left flank. For more than an hour it managed to stave off further Confederate penetration.

Quite simply, after repeated assaults against the Hornets' Nest, the attackers were nearing exhaustion. Spying a small pond, some Mississippi soldiers rushed forward to get a drink. They ignored the dead bodies floating along the water's edge. As one thirsty soldier recalled, 'If the water had been mixed with blood it would have been all the same.'

In the command void left by Johnston's death there was no-one immediately present to re-ignite the faltering assault. A keen-eyed defender observed that the rebels 'marched about hither and yon', seemingly without purpose. A two-regiment Federal counterattack added to the Confederate confusion. With their line bent nearly double, some of the Hornets' Nest defenders began to leak backward toward Pittsburg Landing. They, as well as their leaders, could see the position was becoming untenable. However, Prentiss's last order from Grant had been to hold his position. Thus he did not avail himself of what shortly would become clear was his last opportunity to withdraw.

The great bombardment

For five hours repeated assaults had struck the Hornets' Nest. An Illinois marksman describes the scene. Because of a breeze that dispersed the smoke: 'the Confederate line of battle was in plain sight. It was in the open, in the edge of an old field...It afforded a splendid mark. Even the ramrods could be seen flashing in the air, as the men, while in the act of loading, drew and returned the rammers'.

The 44th Indiana fights in the woods on the Union left. This realistic sketch shows how the combination of smoke and underbrush obscured fields of fire. (Library of Congress)

Harper's Mississippi Battery overlooking the Peach Orchard toward Logan's position at the tree line. (Author's collection)

Among the defenders, Gen. Stephen Hurlbut particularly provided sterling combat leadership. The previous winter, Sherman had advised the hard-drinking lawyer-politician (another of Lincoln's Illinois cronies) to read and study the subject of war. Then he had been amused to overhear Hurlbut practising battalion drill in his room with an experienced lieutenant who knew the proper procedure. Sherman listened while Hurlbut worked on the words of command and the proper tone of voice, ordering phantom units to 'Break from the right, to march to the left!' and 'Battalion Halt! Forward into line'. This earnest preparation paid off in the Hornets' Nest. For hour after hour Hurlbut rode along his line conducting a determined defence, ignoring a spent musket ball that struck him in the arm, showing a cool indifference to a rifle bullet that hit a tree within a few feet of his head. But there was nothing he could do when the Confederates managed to mass a grand battery against his position.

Confederate Brig.Gen. Daniel Ruggles had led his division in support of the general advance from the battle's start until mid-afternoon. Around 3 pm, he gazed across the Duncan Field toward the right centre

of the Hornets' Nest position. He saw a wood line where stood numerous enemy infantry supported by cannon. He appreciated that he confronted a position that the enemy intended to defend obstinately. Rather than rely upon still more naked infantry charges, Ruggles resolved to form a grand battery of artillery with which to bombard the Union position. He sent his staff officers to bring forward every field battery they could find. The resultant artillery concentration produced the greatest volume of fire to date in North America.

Eight batteries and sections from two others, numbering about 53

Alerted by 8:30 am to march toward the battle, Brig.Gen. William 'Bull' Nelson failed to leave Savannah until 1:30 pm. His van troops reached Pittsburg Landing in time to give moral and limited physical support to Grant's men as they repulsed Sunday's last Confederate charge. (National Archives)

field guns, formed in a shallow crescent and opened fire. The range was a mere 500 yards across a level, open field. An Iowa lieutenant who was on the receiving end describes what took place: 'it seemed like a mighty hurricane sweeping everything before it...The great storm of cannon balls made the forest in places fall before its sweep... men and horses were dying, and a blaze of unearthly fire lit up the scene'. The Confederate guns presented a stupendous arc of fire from the rising ground overlooking the Hornets' Nest. They pinned the defenders to the ground.

The bombardment also neutralised the Federal artillery and occupied the defenders' attention, allowing Brig.Gen. Patton Anderson's Brigade of some 1,000 men to march undetected through the thickets screening the right centre of the Hornets' Nest. So thick was the undergrowth that Anderson's company commanders could not even see the length of one of their platoons, a span less than ten yards. However, it became apparent that the bombardment had failed to crush all Federal resistance when Anderson's first assault failed in the face of close-range canister fire. Meanwhile, several Confederate brigades who had been fighting McClernand and Sherman changed facing to bear in against the right rear of the Hornets' Nest. Because of this pressure, when Anderson's men moved forward for a second assault, they saw the defenders throwing down their weapons, waving handkerchiefs, and raising a hastily made white flag. It was surrender.

During the last minutes, the Union soldiers had suffered from serious command confusion. Because they belonged to a variety of commands, it was difficult for any officer to coordinate them. The problem worsened when divisional Gen. W.H.L. Wallace went down with a mortal wound. Some officers thought they should withdraw, others that they should continue to defend or even to advance. In the absence of well co-ordinated infantry support, the Union batteries became vulnerable. The experience of Battery A, 1st Illinois Light Artillery was typical: 'Our infantry support was all broken up into squads and were fighting desperately, while we were firing solid shots and a few shells, having exhausted our canister...the enemy had succeeded in turning our left, and on they came from front and left flank, in solid line to scoop us in. Then Lieut. Wood's voice rang out clear and strong, "Limber to the rear, Get your guns out of this".'

So close did the attacking infantry approach that a gunner could plainly see their brass buttons. During the withdrawal the battery suffered fearfully from point-blank Confederate fire. Initially only four of the six pieces could withdraw; losses among horses and men temporarily immobilised the other two guns. One gun squad lost five of seven men and all but one horse within seconds. Men from the other guns rallied to try to haul this gun to the rear. The surviving horse balked until hit by a bullet which prodded it into action.

OPPOSITE Retreating Federal troops reach the landing while Buell's army arrives across the river. (Library of Congress)

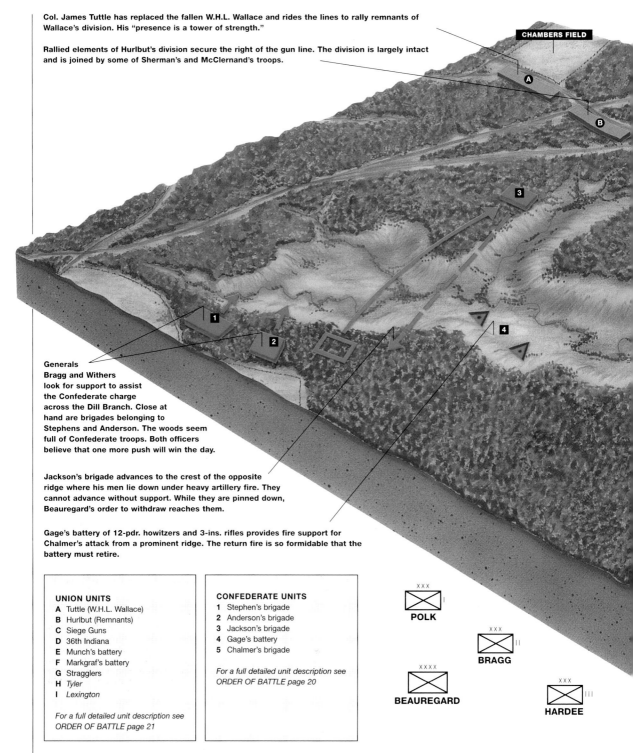

Col. James Tuttle has replaced the fallen W.H.L. Wallace and rides the lines to rally remnants of Wallace's division. His "presence is a tower of strength."

Rallied elements of Hurlbut's division secure the right of the gun line. The division is largely intact and is joined by some of Sherman's and McClernand's troops.

CHAMBERS FIELD

Generals Bragg and Withers look for support to assist the Confederate charge across the Dill Branch. Close at hand are brigades belonging to Stephens and Anderson. The woods seem full of Confederate troops. Both officers believe that one more push will win the day.

Jackson's brigade advances to the crest of the opposite ridge where his men lie down under heavy artillery fire. They cannot advance without support. While they are pinned down, Beauregard's order to withdraw reaches them.

Gage's battery of 12-pdr. howitzers and 3-ins. rifles provides fire support for Chalmer's attack from a prominent ridge. The return fire is so formidable that the battery must retire.

UNION UNITS
A Tuttle (W.H.L. Wallace)
B Hurlbut (Remnants)
C Siege Guns
D 36th Indiana
E Munch's battery
F Markgraf's battery
G Stragglers
H Tyler
I Lexington

For a full detailed unit description see ORDER OF BATTLE page 21

CONFEDERATE UNITS
1 Stephen's brigade
2 Anderson's brigade
3 Jackson's brigade
4 Gage's battery
5 Chalmer's brigade

For a full detailed unit description see ORDER OF BATTLE page 20

POLK

BRAGG

BEAUREGARD

HARDEE

BATTLE OF SHILOH 1862, GRANT HOLDS ON

6 April, 1862, 1730 hours, viewed from the south-east. The Confederates launch one last desperate assault against Grant's last ditch defence over the Dill Branch and by the Tennessee river.

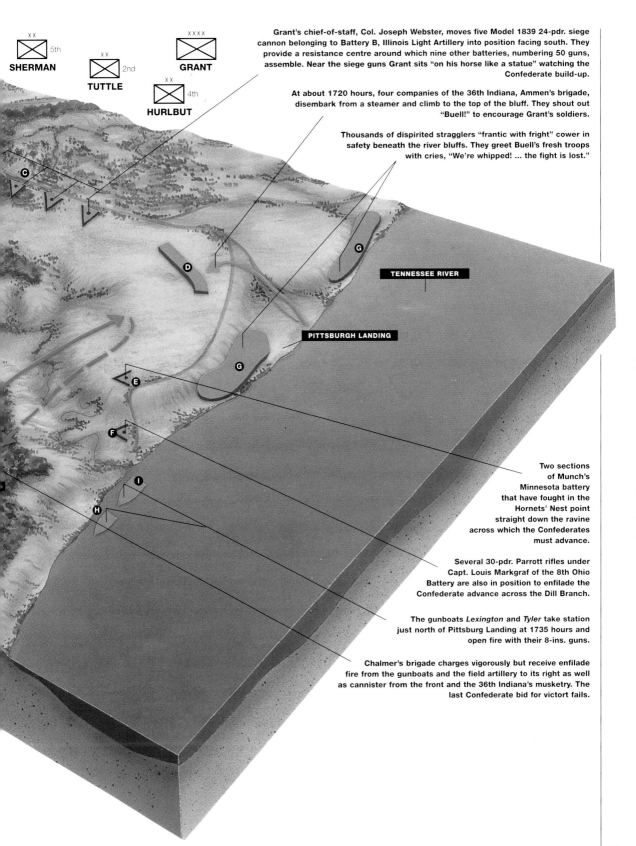

SHERMAN 5th

TUTTLE 2nd

GRANT

HURLBUT 4th

Grant's chief-of-staff, Col. Joseph Webster, moves five Model 1839 24-pdr. siege cannon belonging to Battery B, Illinois Light Artillery into position facing south. They provide a resistance centre around which nine other batteries, numbering 50 guns, assemble. Near the siege guns Grant sits "on his horse like a statue" watching the Confederate build-up.

At about 1720 hours, four companies of the 36th Indiana, Ammen's brigade, disembark from a steamer and climb to the top of the bluff. They shout out "Buell!" to encourage Grant's soldiers.

Thousands of dispirited stragglers "frantic with fright" cower in safety beneath the river bluffs. They greet Buell's fresh troops with cries, "We're whipped! ... the fight is lost."

TENNESSEE RIVER

PITTSBURGH LANDING

Two sections of Munch's Minnesota battery that have fought in the Hornets' Nest point straight down the ravine across which the Confederates must advance.

Several 30-pdr. Parrott rifles under Capt. Louis Markgraf of the 8th Ohio Battery are also in position to enfilade the Confederate advance across the Dill Branch.

The gunboats *Lexington* and *Tyler* take station just north of Pittsburg Landing at 1735 hours and open fire with their 8-ins. guns.

Chalmer's brigade charges vigorously but receive enfilade fire from the gunboats and the field artillery to its right as well as cannister from the front and the 36th Indiana's musketry. The last Confederate bid for victort fails.

67

A somewhat fanciful depiction of Sunday's last rebel assault across the Dill Branch. Union artillery fires in the upper left while Buell's men hasten to the front in the lower right. Spearheaded by their standard bearers, waves of attackers (in reality the lines were much thinner by this time) surge forward while Federal gunboats (in fact there were only two, not the three shown) enfilade the assault. (Library of Congress)

Obeying his last orders from Grant, Prentiss would not budge. He still expected reinforcements and did not fully appreciate that his command stood isolated with both flanks in the air. As one defender later observed, 'We were completely surrounded and whipped, but did not know it.' When it ended after seven hours, only about 2,200 men remained to surrender. The attackers, in turn, had suffered grievous losses during their gallant, but tactically unsound charges. Whether their sacrifice was to earn victory depended upon what happened next.

The last ditch

As Grant understood matters, his battlefield task now reduced itself to surviving until reinforcements arrived. He did not know that the anticipated reinforcements from Wallace and Buell would not arrive in time to save him, and survival depended on the efforts of the five divisions that began the battle. Facing disaster, Grant maintained his composure. He remembered the experience at Fort Donelson, where the Confederate assault had disrupted the attacker as much as the defender. If here at Shiloh the Federal force could hold on, he believed that tomorrow they could counterattack and win the battle.

Grant was confident that his right could hold. Although badly battered, Sherman and McClernand retired slowly to a pre-selected final position along the Hamburg–Savannah Road. They managed to inflict heavy losses on the attacker during this retreat. One of those attackers, belonging to the Orleans Guard Battalion, describes the fighting here. While keeping an eye on the flag-bearer, the soldier noticed that his comrades kept falling: 'Porce down...Gallot down...Coiron, arm shattered...Percy wounded then forty paces...a ragged, stand up volley at the Unionists and they scramble off'. Because of losses and mutual exhaustion, by 3 pm the fight along the Union right had ended.

Elsewhere, the Army of the Tennessee was again in serious trouble. Recalls an Iowa soldier, 'As far as the eye could reach through the woods and over the fields [for] at least a mile, our line of battle [was] in full retreat. Infantry, artillery, wagons, ambulances [were] all rushing to the rear. [It was] a scene of confusion and dismay – an army degenerating into a rout.' To add to the Federal confusion, at this point the battle featured a rare occurrence, a mounted cavalry charge. It occurred when Gen. Polk ordered his cavalry to pursue the remnants fleeing from the Hornets' Nest. Forward went the 1st Mississippi Cavalry for a quarter of a mile. Then they spied a wonderful target 300 yards to the front, a full Union battery with the guns limbered. The cavalry charged at the gallop and overran the battery capturing intact four 10-pdr. Parrotts and one brass 6-pounder.

Earlier in the afternoon, Grant's chief-of-staff, Col. Joseph Webster, had received Grant's permission to prepare a position near Pittsburg Landing on a steep ridge overlooking the Dill Branch. By the time Prentiss surrendered, Webster had collected some 50 artillery pieces to occupy a half-mile-long position. Anchoring it was a battery of 24-pdr. siege guns that had been brought to Pittsburg Landing in the optimistic belief they would be needed to batter Confederate entrenchments at Corinth. About 4,000 semi-organised infantry from a variety of commands supported the gun line. A Michigan private recalls that his 'proud army of Donelson was crouching like whipped curs in a small circular line'. After a day of punishment and retreat, it required considerable valour to even try to hold this

Brigadier-General James Chalmers' Brigade struggled across the Dill Branch into the teeth of the Federal artillery defence. (US Army Military History Institute)

The gunboats *Lexington* (shown here) and *Tyler* enfiladed Chalmers' assault. (Library of Congress)

line. A battery commander relates that the men sensed that this was the last ditch, a position that had to be held if the army were to survive.

Behind the gun line, thousands of officers and men thronged to safety below the crest of the river bank. Some officers rode among these dispirited men in a vain effort to rally them. At dusk, when Brig.Gen. William Nelson of Buell's army arrived at the landing, he rode through the packed crowd waving his hat and shouting 'Fall in, boys, fall in and follow me. We shall whip them yet'. Finding that words did no good, Nelson set to with the flat of his sword. Nothing could force the badly frightened men back into the ranks. The ones who had seen terrible slaughter up close wanted no more to do with it. Their experiences hardly inspired those who had run at the beginning to rally now. It was a doleful introduction to battle for Nelson's men. As they shouldered their way through the milling shirkers and climbed the river bluff from the landing, voices shouted out, 'For God's sake, don't go out there or you will be killed.' But Nelson's men marched on and their arrival lifted the morale of the men occupying Grant's final defensive position.

Across the lines, Bragg appreciated that with the sun setting, time was of the essence. He issued orders to press the Confederate advantage, to 'Sweep everything forward...drive the enemy into the river'. Polk shared his view and he too set about urging the Army of the Mississippi to renew its advance. But the convergence of so many Confederate troops upon the Hornets' Nest had created an enormous snarl that took time to unravel. In the belief that victory was theirs and because they were acutely hungry, ever more soldiers had left the ranks to loot the captured camps. Moreover, the attackers were much fatigued and had suffered

Confederate Col. Ben Helm's erroneous report that Buell was en route to Decatur, Alabama, persuaded Beauregard that he had ample time to gobble up Grant's isolated army during a second day of battle. Helm had married Abraham Lincoln's half-sister, and the two men were close friends. (Tennessee State Library and Archives)

The conditions at Pittsburg Landing appalled Maj.Gen. Don Carlos Buell. Then and thereafter he was certain that his army's arrival saved the Army of the Tennessee. (National Archives)

heavy losses. The obstacle before them, the Dill Branch, was a rugged ravine, steep and wooded. Nevertheless, at around 5:30 pm, amidst the onset of heavy explosions as the US Navy gunboats *Lexington* and *Tyler* opened fire with their large-bore guns, the Confederate line again went forward.

The physical stamina required to attack at this point was enormous. Like most of the day's attacks, this last assault was an uncoordinated affair. While Chalmers' Brigade attacked near the river, Jackson's men went forward, felt the Union artillery fire, and withdrew behind a sheltering crestline. Chalmers' assault crossed the Dill Branch only to collapse against heavy artillery fire from the front and enfilade fire from the gunboats. A Federal eyewitness recalls, 'the enemy appeared on the crest...but were cut to pieces by the steady and murderous fire of our artillery'. Confederate division commander Brig.Gen. Jones Withers was preparing to send forward additional troops when he saw Jackson's Brigade retreating. He was on the verge of arresting Jackson for cowardice when, to his great surprise, he learned that Jackson was responding to orders from Beauregard. 'Old Bory' was ordering a retreat! When Bragg learned this he was stunned. Then and thereafter he believed it a war-losing error.

When Beauregard had learned of the death of Sidney Johnston and his own accession to army command, he was at a field headquarters well behind the battle line. He remained there for another 90 minutes and what he saw was disheartening. Confederate stragglers, shirkers, and numerous wounded milled about in great confusion. A staff officer reported to him that over a third of the army was scattered away from their units. Another message came via the base back at Corinth that Buell's Army was marching on Decatur, Alabama. This meant that Grant would receive no help from Buell and thus the day's business could be completed tomorrow. Beauregard did not know the report was mistaken. At 5:30 pm Beauregard moved even further to the rear to establish a headquarters near Shiloh Church. He then issued orders to call off the fighting for the day.

In contrast, Ulysses Grant was right at the point of decision during the last rebel charge. According to an eyewitness, he sat on his horse chewing a cigar 'imperturbably' even while a cannon shot beheaded one of his staff ten feet away. Another staffer saw him gazing toward the retiring Confederates after their final repulse. He was speaking, as if to himself. Uncertain, the staffer rode closer and heard Grant mutter, 'Not beaten yet by a damn sight.' It was a sentiment he reiterated when meeting Sherman later that evening. Sherman commented that, 'we've had the devil's own day, haven't we?' Grant replied, 'Yes, lick 'em tomorrow, though.' And so Sunday's fighting ended.

'A night of horrors'

The night was a testing time for the men on both sides of the battle line. At Pittsburg Landing, regimental bands played for most of the long, rainy night in an effort to hearten and rally the hundreds of dispirited soldiers sheltered along the river bank. Having been driven from their camps, Grant's men had to endure great discomfort without recourse to their tents, blankets, food, and supplies. The always primitive medical service collapsed completely, inundated by far more wounded than

anyone had expected, and forced to operate after losing most of their surgical supplies. However, soldiers could take heart in the fact that overnight substantial reinforcements belonging to Buell's army reached Pittsburg Landing to take position behind the Federal gun line. On the opposite flank, Lew Wallace's division finally arrived after a bungled, roundabout march to provide another fresh fighting force.

Across the lines the Confederate soldiers believed they had won a major victory. Plunder from the Union camps partially offset the chill rain that fell. Shirkers continued to collect the bounty. One officer complained that by midnight 'half our army was straggling back to Corinth loaded down with belts, sashes, swords, officers' uniforms, Yankee letters, daguerreotypes of Yankee sweethearts...some on Yankee mules and horses, some on foot, some on the ground prostrate with Cincinnati whiskey'. Even those who had served manfully until nightfall now availed themselves of the opportunity to plunder. Sam Watkins recalls that 'The

Fifteen companies of US regulars fought in Buell's army at Shiloh. The captain commanding the 15th US Infantry proudly reported the special discipline that characterised the regulars: 'Three times we charged upon the foe, the last time with the bayonet, capturing a battery. My officers displayed great bravery, and gallantly conducted their companies in the hottest of the engagement with the regularity of a drill, and the men were cool, steady, and obedient, well exemplifying their discipline.' (National Archives)

soldiers had passed through the Yankee camps and saw all the good things that they had to eat...it was but a short time before every soldier was rummaging to see what he could find.'

The officer corps was over-confident, sharing Beauregard's belief that the morning would see them triumph. One vigilant rebel dissented. Bedford Forrest, who on this field continued to show his potential as one of the war's best tactical leaders, sent a scouting party dressed in blue uniforms into the enemy line. They saw Buell's men disembarking from transports. Forrest reported this intelligence to Hardee and Breckinridge. He added that either the army should attack this night and complete the victory or abandon the field. Hardee did nothing beyond sending Forrest to inform Beauregard. However, because of sloppy staff work, no-one could lead Forrest to Beauregard's headquarters. In fact, Beauregard was comfortably ensconced in Sherman's tent, but had failed to inform his staff of this change of headquarters. Consequently, the rebel commander-in-chief remained ignorant that the tables had turned: instead of completing his offensive against a battered enemy, tomorrow 'Old Bory's' Army of Mississippi would have to defend against a near overwhelming force.

Grant spent a miserable night among his troops. Driven from his headquarters by the piteous cries of the wounded, he tried to rest outdoors. He experienced a clear demonstration that the rains could fall on general and private alike. Still, the arrival of fresh troops heartened him. Recalling the lesson of Fort Donelson, Grant reasoned that here too, the side that struck first would gain a great morale advantage. When young James McPherson of his staff queried whether he intended to retreat, Grant replied decisively, 'No! I propose to attack at daylight and whip them'. However, the combination of his own fatigue and the army's confused alignment kept him from issuing specific instructions. Unbelievably, he did not meet with Buell, who had arrived at Pittsburg Landing and was supervising the disembarkation of his own army. Buell, in turn, was contemptuous of the fact that the Army of the Tennessee seemed to be a defeated force. Consequently, while planning his own offensive he made no effort to meet with Grant. This abject failure of communication by the two Federal army commanders saved the rebel army from destruction.

Brigadier-General Patrick Cleburne would become one of the South's outstanding combat leaders. During Monday's action, Cleburne's brigade suffered heavy losses when Bragg committed it to an ill-advised counterattack. (Tennessee State Library and Archives)

Counter-offensive

On the morning of 7 April, sparked by 25,000 reinforcements, the Union armies pushed forward all along the line. It was not a well co-ordinated advance. Grant and Buell's failure to communicate with one another resulted in a disjointed series of attacks similar to those of the Confederates the previous day. Adjacent attacking brigades failed to co-ordinate their manoeuvres, and units became disorganised in the tangled terrain. Entire regiments and batteries fired into friendly troops. There was little tactical finesse, but rather numerous frontal pushes that relied on weight of numbers alone.

The action began at 5 am when Nelson's Division emerged from behind Dills Branch. They gained ground easily against a surprised foe, until Buell committed a major blunder by ordering the division to halt. Buell wanted to utilise the elbow room Nelson had gained to deploy the balance of his force, but by the time the deployment was complete three

Colonel William B. Hazen commanded Buell's 19th Brigade. His strict discipline, attention to detail, and insistence on regular drill converted his midwestern volunteers into an excellent combat unit. (National Archives)

As had been the case with the Union artillery on Sunday, on Monday the Confederate artillery provided knots of resistance around which the defending infantry formed. A 12-pdr. howitzer of Bankhead's Tennessee Battery. (Author's collection)

hours had passed. By then, the Confederates were alert and in position, and stern fighting replaced easy progress. While Buell's army carried the assault in the centre and left, Lew Wallace's Division advanced on the Union right. So battered were Grant's other divisions from Sunday's fight that they managed to occupy a mere quarter-mile front between Wallace and Buell.

The sounds of Buell's offensive woke Beauregard in his tent. From the volume of Union fire it was clear that Buell's army was not far distant. Yet his tactical direction for this day was little different from the previous day. He remained at his headquarters and sent staff officers to urge reserves to march to the sound of the heaviest firing.

In some cases Beauregard's men occupied positions defined by the limits of the previous day's advance. Other units had retired at dusk the previous day to the captured tent line in order to rest and refit. There was a general loss of command and control and Bishop Polk was the worst offender. He allowed Clark's division to remain on the ground they occupied at nightfall, while his other division under Cheatham retired all the way back to the Confederate start line in order to find ammunition and food. Showing he preferred personal comfort over his troops' welfare – a tendency he exhibited again at Chickamauga – Polk accompanied his soldiers to the rear. Thus, the Confederate centre was neither tied into any kind of tactical order, nor was its commander present when the bluecoats struck. Worse, few officers had taken measures to ensure that their men had renewed their ammunition, even though they camped in the middle of an ample supply of captured Union materiel. Furthermore, nightfall had permitted hungry soldiers to leave the ranks, and many did not return in time for the second day's battle. General Pat Cleburne, whose brigade's discipline exceeded most, had started the battle with nearly 2,700 men. For the second day's battle he could collect only some 800.

Illustrative of rebel disorder was the experience of a Confederate staff officer who had the duty of rallying men scattered by the previous day's combat. He was one among many assigned this duty and easily collected 1,000 soldiers belonging to some half-dozen different regiments. Although they were willing to fight, there was not a single field officer among them. The fact that one staffer found 1,000 willing stragglers hints at the far greater number of unwilling stragglers who were unavailable for the second day's fight. Indeed, a Tennessee colonel received a large complement of stragglers to support his regiment. He complained that they 'demonstrated very clearly this morning that they had strayed from their own regiments because they did not want to fight, and that they still would not fight'.

Such was the disorder on the Confederate left that Col. Preston Pond's Brigade alone confronted Lew Wallace's entire division. Pond wrote, 'I regarded the position as perilous, and would no doubt have been cut off or cut to pieces but for the cool, intrepid, and gallant conduct of Cpt. Ketchum.' Ketchum's Alabama Battery held off Lew Wallace's infantry long enough for Pond to withdraw. Indeed, Ketchum's performance was the first of a series of distinguished rearguard actions fought by the Confederate artillery during the second day of battle. However, contributing to the rebel defence was the fact that Lew Wallace displayed Buell-like caution by ordering his division to hold in place until he secured support from neighbouring units on his left flank. His division would suffer only 43 killed and 257 wounded during Monday's fighting.

Partially compensating for the Army of the Mississippi's disorder was the fact that most of the fresh Union soldiers who fought on Monday had never faced combat. They repeated the mistakes of the previous day. One of Lew Wallace's men, Private Elisha Stockwell, describes entering the firing line and being told not to shoot until his regiment's skirmishers had cleared the front. Stockwell had to hold the musket of his adjacent comrade to keep him from firing prematurely. Then, 'We were ordered to fire, and as soon as I let go of Ned's gun, he stuck it up in the air, shut both eyes, and fired at the tree tops... Schnider did the same. But Schnider was in rear rank and behind Curly and he cut a lock of Curly's hair off just above the ear, and burned his neck.' After enduring an unnerving shelling (probably from Ketchum's Battery) Stockwell describes his regiment's charge: 'We had lost all formation, and were rushing down the road like a mob...We stopped...and I got behind a small tree. I could see the little puffs of smoke at the top of the hill on the other side some forty rods from us, and I shot at those puffs. The brush was so thick I couldn't see the Rebs, but loaded and fired at the smoke until a grape shot came through the tree and knocked me flat as I was putting the cap on my gun. I thought my arm was gone, but I rolled on my right side and looked at my arm and couldn't see anything wrong with it, so got to my feet...and saw the Rebs coming down hill just like we had.'

All along the Confederate line, after recovering from their initial shock, the rebels responded to the Federal offensive with fierce coun- terattacks of the type Private Stockwell confronted. In part, this

Hazen's Brigade charges during Monday's battle. Hazen is the mounted officer far left in front of the battle line. Nelson is among the group of mounted officers behind the lines and is facing to the rear toward Buell, who, in turn, is in lower right with hand raised. The 9th Indiana is to Hazen's left. (Library of Congress)

aggressiveness was due to the front-line soldiers' belief that they were still on the offensive. In addition, bellicose leaders such as Hardee and Bragg were determined to conduct an active defence. But Bragg did not seem able to grasp tactics. Showing he had learned nothing from the previous day, he ordered Cleburne's Brigade to charge. Cleburne describes what took place: 'There was a very thick undergrowth here of young trees, which prevented my men from seeing any distance, yet offered them no protection from the storm of bullets and grape shot that swept through it. I could not see what was going on to my right or left, but my men were dropping all around before the fire of an unseen foe.'

Likewise, on the second day of fighting Beauregard's conduct revealed him to be out of touch with Civil War battlefield reality. Around 10 am Grant's soldiers were pressing hard against the Confederate left flank. In order to relieve the pressure, Beauregard chose a Napoleonic response by ordering Col. John Wharton's Texas Rangers to charge the Union flank. To manoeuvre, Wharton had to form the Rangers in a narrow column. He tried to gain the Union flank by leading them through the woods and down the side of a ravine. Upon mounting the ravine's far side Wharton saw two deployed enemy regiments advancing toward him. They 'opened a very disastrous fire upon us, killing and wounding many and disabling my horse'. Wharton tried to maintain his position until his entire regiment arrived. But movement through the woods was so difficult that the regiment was strung out over a 400-yard span. The head of the column could not endure the fire and recoiled. For the remainder of this combat, Wharton dismounted his Rangers and fought them as infantry skirmishers. 'I regret exceedingly', he later reported, that the difficult terrain 'deprived the Rangers from charging the enemy with effect' at any point during the two-day battle. The Rangers' one abortive charge cost them most of their 66 casualties along with 56 dead horses.

On Sunday Grant's artillery had been the keystone of the defence. Likewise on Monday, artillery on the defensive showed its power. Having thwarted Lew Wallace's initial advance, Ketchum's Alabama gunners continued to serve as the proverbial finger in the dike. The battery performed a model fighting retreat by deploying on rising ground, firing until the enemy drew near, and then retiring to the next rise to the rear. Then it came time for a hard stand. Ordered by Bragg to help some infantry who were on the verge of being overwhelmed, Ketchum advanced 'the battery in a gallop on a road bringing us on the enemy's left, we came into battery, discharging canister from our six pieces at a distance of 40 or 50 yards, checking his advance and driving him back in the thicket, our troops rallying again'.

In spite of such conduct, slowly the entire Union battle line moved forward. One of Buell's officers described advancing toward Hurlbut's former campsite where 'The enemy's infantry, concealed by tents, behind trees, and in dense undergrowth, opened a terrific fire on our whole line'. The experience of the 6th Indiana Infantry was typical. The regiment, serving in Rousseau's Brigade, began advancing at 7 am. Arriving at the fringe of an open field, it received a heavy fire of canister and musketry, as well as some errant shelling from a friendly battery. The colonel ordered his men to lie down and return the enemy fire. Twice they saw the opposing enemy flag go down. After a prolonged musketry duel, the rebels retired. The 6th Indiana moved forward until again encountering a severe canister and musketry fire. Buell had been forced to leave all but two of his batteries back at Savannah. Fortunately, at this point one of the two arrived at the trot. 'We opened ranks for our artillery to pass through and then closed up for the coming struggle,' reports the 6th Indiana's colonel. Faced with a Confederate counterattack, the 'regiment stood up and fired 20 rounds so rapidly as to make a steady storm of musketry and compelled the enemy to halt. Seeing this, I ordered the regiment forward about 100 yards, when the enemy gave way'.

When the defending rebels faltered, some officers performed miracles to rally them. Exceptional was the conduct of Lt. Sandidge of Ruggles' staff. Seeing a regiment refusing to charge, Sandidge rode over, seized its colours, held them high overhead and called for the men to follow. Waving the banner, he spurred his horse and 'charged over the brow of the hill amid a shower of leaden hail from the enemy'. Sandidge's conduct stirred the infantry forward, but their counterattack collapsed against superior numbers.

On Buell's front some of the hardest fighting occurred in the area of the Peach Field. Here Confederate Gen. Withers formed a line along the Hamburg–Purdy Road and awaited the advance of Nelson's division. Nelson's centre brigade, Col. Sanders Bruce's four Union-loyal Kentucky regiments, advanced toward the orchard only to receive severe enfilade fire from the Washington Artillery of New Orleans. When enemy

At 5 am, Nelson's fresh division leads Buell's advance. An hour later, serious combat has resumed. On the opposite flank, Lew Wallace's division attacks Pond's brigade at 6.30 am and makes cautious progress. Meanwhile, Crittenden's division joins in on Nelson's left at 7 am followed by Rousseau's division an hour later. Some 7,000 effectives belonging to Sherman, McClernand and Hurlbut advance at 10 am to link with Wallace and Buell. By noon the Federals have pushed the Confederates back to a second line where the fighting continues until 3 pm by which time Beauregard orders a general retreat.

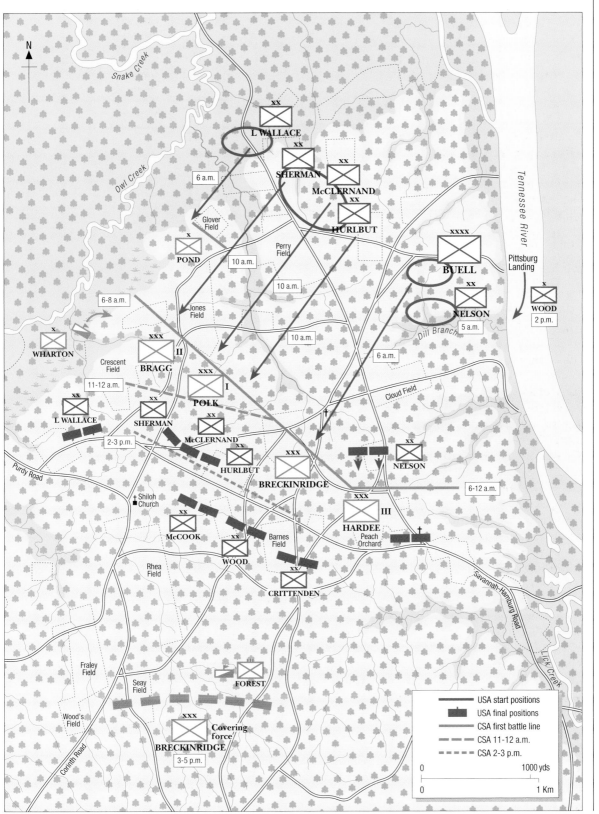

N

Snake Creek

Owl Creek

Tennessee River

xx
L WALLACE

6 a.m.

Glover
Field

xx
SHERMAN

xx
McCLERNAND

xx
HURLBUT

x
POND

Perry
Field

10 a.m.

xxxx
BUELL

Pittsburg
Landing

xx
NELSON

5 a.m.

x
WOOD

2 p.m.

6-8 a.m.

Jones
Field

10 a.m.

10 a.m.

6 a.m.

Dill Branch

x
WHARTON

Crescent
Field

xxx II
BRAGG

11-12 a.m.

xxx I
POLK

Cloud Field

†

xx
L WALLACE

xx
SHERMAN

2-3 p.m.

xx
McCLERNAND

xx
HURLBUT

xxx
BRECKINRIDGE

xx
NELSON

6-12 a.m.

Purdy Road

† Shiloh
Church

xxx III
HARDEE

Peach
Orchard

†

xx
McCOOK

Barnes
Field

xx
WOOD

Rhea
Field

xx
CRITTENDEN

Savannah-Hamburg Road

Lick Creek

Fraley
Field

Seay
Field

iii
FOREST

Wood's
Field

xxx
BRECKINRIDGE

Covering
force

3-5 p.m.

Corinth Road

▬▬▬	USA start positions
▰▰	USA final positions
───	CSA first battle line
▬ ▬ ▬	CSA 11-12 a.m.
▪ ▪ ▪	CSA 2-3 p.m.

0   1000 yds

0   1 Km

musketry joined in Bruce's men retired. This left Hazen's Brigade isolated on Nelson's right flank. At this time, about 10 am, a fierce rebel counterattack bore in against Hazen's men.

The 9th Indiana was one of 16 Indiana regiments to fight at Shiloh. (National Archives)

Ordered by Beauregard to charge in conjunction with Breckinridge, Gen. Hardee could do little to co-ordinate the charge, but he did ride forward on his beautiful black charger to inspire his men. With a tremendous cheer, the 2nd Confederate spearheaded the assault. The rebels shrugged off the effect of the enemy's canister fire and closed in, taunting their foes with shouts of 'Bull Run! Bull Run!' The sight unnerved some of Hazen's men and they recoiled. But Buell was just behind them and he ordered an immediate counter-attack from the recently rallied soldiers of Bruce's Brigade. A brief, close-range combat took place in the underbrush. Outnumbered, the Confederates yielded. 'They run!' shouted some of Bruce's men, and the entire blue battle line took up the cry. A 'wild pursuit' took place, bringing Bruce's Kentucky bluecoats and Hazen's men up against the Confederate Washington Artillery. They overran the battery, capturing three guns, and argued ever after about who had accomplished this feat. But the charge had disorganised the two

The 14th Wisconsin Volunteers charges and captures a rebel battery during Monday's counter-offensive. (Library of Congress)

spearheading Federal brigades. When a sister brigade mistakenly fired into their rear, and another Confederate battery opened fire, Hazen's Brigade retreated.

Throughout it all, Gen. Hardee provided inspirational front-line leadership. An admiring eyewitness writes, 'he seemed to be the master spirit, giving all orders and seeing that they were properly executed'. Hardee's horse received a wound, and at least two bullets ripped through his coat. Having just witnessed a gallant attack fail, his fighting blood was up. Consequently, when he perceived that the 2nd Texas was not carrying it's weight he became angry. Hardee sent an aide to inform the unit that he would call them a 'pack of cowards' if they did not do their duty. A Texas officer, hiding behind a tree with some of his men, replied that they did not care a damn what Hardee might call them! Shortly thereafter, the regiment broke and fled to the rear.

Undaunted, other Confederate units charged forward against Nelson's men. They drove back Nelson's third brigade commanded by Col. Ammen. Here, 'The storm of musket ball, canister shot, and shell...was truly awful,' noted a Union officer. It seemed to Nelson that his entire line was on the verge of breaking and that only Terrill's Battery H, 5th Artillery stood between victory and defeat. Indeed, Terrill's regulars had suffered fearfully, with so many gunners shot that Terrill himself manned a gun. Nelson shouted to the 6th Ohio that the battery 'must not be taken.' Soldiers went forward to help serve the guns. Firing deliberately, Terrill's regulars repulsed repeated Confederate charges. The Confederate counterattack had shot its bolt. As Brigadier Chalmers, who had performed with maniacal energy to organise the counterattack, reported, 'I called upon my brigade to make one more effort, but they seemed too much exhausted to make the attempt.' Union Col. William Hazen, showing on this field that he was developing a fine tactical talent, sensed the moment and ordered his drummers to beat the charge. The ensuing bayonet attack drove the

Confederates back three-quarters of a mile.

Overall, it was becoming apparent that the Confederate line could barely be maintained. The fiercest Federal pressure converged on the area of Shiloh Church. By early afternoon infantry resistance along the Confederate left centre had collapsed. Too many officers had been killed or wounded, and the soldiers were exhausted. Left alone was Stanford's Mississippi Battery. At 300-yard range, Stanford's six guns opened fire against charging infantry. Stanford relates, 'Large gaps were made by every gun at each discharge. Three regimental flags being in full view, I gave the order to point at them, and soon had the satisfaction of seeing two of them to the ground, both being raised again. One was again cut down'. The Union infantry implacably pressed through the canister fire. When they had closed to 75 yards, Stanford gave orders to limber up. It was too late. A gunner describes, 'Most of the horses were killed, and those living were so badly tangled it was impossible to get them in order under the heavy fire of Minie balls'. The attackers, volunteers and US regulars belonging to Rousseau's Brigade, captured four cannon and six caissons.

Shortly thereafter, around 2 pm, Col. Jordan commented to Beauregard that the Confederate line resembled a soaked lump of sugar, still holding together but ready to dissolve momentarily. Beauregard concurred. At 3:30 pm the retreat began. A 2,000-man rearguard commanded by Breckinridge covered the withdrawal. There was no effective pursuit that day. As an Iowa soldier wrote in his diary, 'The two armies are like two tenacious bull dogs. They have grappled and fought until both are exhausted and worn out. One has crawled away to lie down and the other one cannot follow.'

Terrill's 5th US Artillery employed move and fire tactics to support Buell's counter-offensive. The battery's two 10-pdr. Parrott rifles expended 26 time fuse shells, 11 percussion shells, 11 case shot, and 28 canister; its four light 12-pdr. smoothbores expended 53 solid shot, 19 shell, 65 spherical case, and 29 canister. This photo, taken in the east, shows the crew of a 10-pdr. Parrott rifle at drill. Examining the field the day after the battle, a soldier came upon five dead Confederates. They had been behind a log and all in a row. A cannon ball had raked them as they crouched: 'One of them had his head taken off. One had been struck at the right shoulder and his chest lay open. One had been cut in two at the bowels and nothing held the carcass together but the spine. One had been hit at the thighs and the legs were torn from the body. The fifth and last one was piled up into a mass of skull, arms, some toes, and the remains of a butternut suit. Just a few feet from where they lay the [6-pdr.] cannon ball had struck a large tree and lodged.' (National Archives)

AFTERMATH

'The terrible scenes are indelibly
fixed in my memory'

The sun rose on 8 April to illuminate a sight never before seen on the North American continent. It was a scene resulting from the merger of improved firepower with outdated Napoleonic tactics: 'The bodies of dead horses and wrecks of wagons, caissons, guns and all kinds of war implements, were strewn over the battlefield. The dead were lying in every conceivable shape. Some had fallen with guns fast in their hands, others had...sought the shelter of logs and trees, and laid down to die.' Around the Hornets' Nest one soldier recalled that the fallen lay so thick that he could have walked across the field on the bodies of dead rebels. It was a hot day and the bodies began to decompose. Union burial parties, fortified by whisky to endure the work, dug trenches and filled them with the dead. Simple, hand-carved, wooden boards marked the grave sites: here, '125 rebels'; there, '35 Union.' The work seemed endless.

Meanwhile, North and South, the thousands of wounded overwhelmed the primitive abilities of the care providers. The Confederates tried to haul their wounded back to Corinth aboard miserable, unsprung wagons. They left behind hundreds of men too injured to move. Around Pittsburg Landing, every tent, house, and wagon was choked with wounded men. As quickly as possible, steamers shipped them away from the battlefield. But even aboard the transports intense misery reigned: 'The scene...was heart-rending. Men wounded and mangled in every conceivable way...some with arms, legs, and their jaws shot off, bleeding to death and...no surgeons to attend us.' At nearby Savannah, the Federal post commander informed his wife, 'You can have no conception of the amount of suffering here. Men lay out in stables and die without their wounds dressed.' The scarcity of medical officers, their general ignorance, and the poor organisation that characterised casualty clearing and medical care condemned hundreds to slow death.

The battle of Shiloh had been fought between two raw armies. By and large, given that they were new to their trade, both sides had done extremely well and had displayed a determined stubbornness that typified the western battles during the war's first three years. The inexperience of officers and men alike, coupled with the difficult terrain, had reduced the battle to a series of disjointed frontal charges. The absence of tactical acumen contributed to the heavy losses. Grant's Army of the Tennessee had 87 officers and 1,426 men killed; 336 officers and 6,265 men wounded; and 115 officers and 2,318 men missing or captured. This total of 10,944 represented a loss rate of about one in four. Buell's Army of the Ohio suffered 2,103 casualties for a grand total of 13,047. The Army of the Mississippi lost 1,723 killed, 8,012 wounded, and 959 missing or captured out of an effective total of 38,733 men. This was a loss rate of nearly 28 per cent.

Polk's First Corps artillery had 139 out of 347 battery horses killed. This extraordinary mortality forced the gunners to abandon nine guns and 19 caissons on the field. However, they did retreat with 13 Federal cannon which were superior to the types they left behind. (National Archives)

Grant's army had a hard nucleus of soldiers who had fought at Fort Donelson. The balance of the Union and Confederate troops that fought at Shiloh were no better trained, organised, or experienced than the armies who had fought at Bull Run. Once Buell's and Wallace's men joined the battle, the battle of Shiloh saw about 100,000 men engaged, a number twice the size of the combined forces at Bull Run. Yet the western armies at Shiloh, in comparison to the eastern armies at Bull Run, fought three times longer, suffered five times the losses, and did not rout from the field. To put this performance in historical perspective, the American armies at Shiloh experienced a percentage loss about equal to that of the battle of Waterloo. Shiloh's grim total exceeded the sum of all American casualties suffered during the entire Revolution, War of 1812, and Mexican War.

At least one Union soldier expressed surprise that losses had not been heavier. Fifteen-year-old Elisha Stockwell had fought bravely during his first battle. He had received two wounds in addition to an accidental bayonet cut from a fallen comrade. After the battle he complained to the 60 per cent of his company who had survived the battle that he was disappointed so many rebels got away. He had supposed that once a battle began everyone continued firing until all on one side or the other were killed!

Because the two-day battle featured first one army and then the other storming one another's position, there was a great exchange of equipment. On Sunday the Confederates captured about 33 artillery pieces. The next day Buell's men captured 20 artillery pieces, many of which had been lost by Grant the previous day. The Army of the Tennessee also captured or recaptured ten cannon. Overall, the Confederates probably came out three guns ahead, but in addition several Confederate batteries exchanged superior Union ordnance for their own guns. The same occurred with small arms. Breckinridge's Reserve Corps alone carried from the field 1,393 small arms in addition to those exchanged on the field. The entire Confederate army returned to Corinth carrying five captured regimental colours and 20 Stars and Stripes.

Confederate generals had led from the front and they suffered accordingly. Sidney Johnston, George Johnson (Kentucky's Confederate governor whose horse was killed beneath him on Sunday and served on foot in the ranks on Monday) and Brig.Gen. Adley Gladden all died. Corps commanders Hardee and Breckinridge were both wounded; Bragg had two horses shot out from under him; divisional General Withers lost three horses and received a slight wound, while fellow divisional commander Clark received a severe wound; brigade commanders Hindman, B.R. Johnson, and Bowen received serious injuries.

This hints at how badly both armies were cut up. The day after the battle Bragg reported that his men's condition was 'horrible' with the troops 'utterly disorganised and demoralised'. General Breckinridge echoed this sentiment, describing his command as 'thoroughly worn-out' from fatigue, false alarms, and exposure. Confederate trains and artillery had great difficulty retreating over clogged and muddy roads. An aggressive Union pursuit would have captured much valuable ordnance.

Grant's army was in almost as bad a shape as its foe. The presence of Buell's relatively fresh force, however, as well as the navy's ability to rush supplies to Pittsburg Landing made a great difference in the speed of the Federal recovery. Nonetheless, so hard had been the blow, that Halleck sent orders for Grant to 'avoid another battle'. In the meantime, Grant undertook all the precautions that he should have taken before the battle. He issued detailed orders for each brigade to post men along the front to provide warning should the enemy reappear. Cavalry pickets were to be well advanced, cross-roads and fords observed. Brigade commanders were to fell trees to make breastworks and the underbrush within 200 yards of each camp was to be cleared so no enemy could draw near undetected.

Reflecting upon the battle, many Northerners began to think that their superior officers had badly let them down. Criticism started with the man at the top. An Iowa soldier spoke for many when he wrote, 'I think Gen. Grant fell short of his duty. He knew or might have known, that the rebels were coming to attack us, and he staid [sic] at Savannah until after they commenced their work.' One soldier gathered up gossip and concluded that he spoke 'the sentiments of the army when I say that Gen. Grant is responsible for much of the terrible sacrifice of life on the 6th'. Another soldier spoke more bluntly, claiming that Grant 'was hated and despised by all the men and cursed ever since'. Such feelings quickly worked their way into the press as families shared with their local newspapers the letters they received from their soldier sons. Simultaneously, war correspondents echoed their sentiments. One typical reporter wrote that the commanding general had been 'quietly snoozing down at Savannah...and did not git on the field till after noon; and then was drunk'.

Afterwards, Grant lamely defended his decision not to fortify his campsite saying that 'drill and discipline were worth more to our men

On the field at Shiloh, and afterwards during his rearguard action at Fallen Timbers, Bedford Forrest demonstrated his unique talents that were to make him one of the most feared Confederate warriors. At Fallen Timbers two shots killed Forrest's horse and a rifle bullet seriously wounded him in the hip, making him the last casualty of the battle of Shiloh. (Tennessee State Library and Archives)

than fortifications'. This disingenuously overlooks the fact that his raw troops could have acquired drill and discipline while digging breastworks. The fact is, Grant never suspected an enemy strike against his camp. Civilians living behind his lines had reported to probing Confederate cavalry that the Union army had not dug in, and this helped encourage Johnston to launch his attack. Over-confident and ill-prepared, Grant was most fortunate to win the battle.

When Grant had arrived on the field, one of his first messages was sent to Buell urging him to hasten to the battle. Reinforcements would 'possibly save the day', Grant wrote. Then and thereafter, Buell believed that he and his command had indeed saved the day. After the war, the two fought a pamphlet war about credit and blame. Caustically, Buell inquired how an army leader could allow his force to be so woefully unprepared given the known presence of a large enemy force only 20 miles away. Buell recalled the panicky scene around the landing on the evening of 6 April and contrasted it with the conduct of his own men as they shouldered their way through the hordes of demoralised soldiers to occupy the final defensive line. In fact, Grant's men had repulsed the last rebel attack largely unaided. However, in the absence of Buell's reinforcements, the Union force would have been unable to attack on the second day and might not have been able to hold off renewed Confederate assaults.

Indeed, had Grant suffered defeat the consequences are incalculable. Almost certainly, defeat at Shiloh would have blocked Grant's subsequent career. Sherman's incredible negligence would have likewise thwarted his rise. The two major field commanders in the ultimately successful 1864 offensive would never have reached superior command. To his credit, Grant learned from the experience. Never again would he make the same mistakes. In the short term, Halleck effectively relieved Grant from command for the next campaign. Worse would have occurred had not Abraham Lincoln interceded. When politicians in Washington demanded Grant's removal, Lincoln replied, 'I can't spare this man; he fights.'

In contrast to attitudes toward Grant were the feelings directed

Major-General Henry Halleck commanded a sprawling department composed of Missouri, Kansas, Ohio, Kentucky, and Tennessee. An able administrator with occasional strategic insight, he was no field commander. Shiloh's casualty list appalled him and he blamed Grant. (National Archives)

BELOW **After the battle the dead, bloated horses made an awful stench. Union soldiers burn dead horses near the Peach Orchard. (Library of Congress)**

toward Buell. In the minds of many, Buell's generalship had saved the army. Subsequent events would prove Buell to be an indifferent general at best. Somewhat surprisingly, Sherman came out of the battle with his reputation bolstered. Halleck praised him, writing that he had 'saved the fortune of the day' on the sixth. In fact, although Sherman had displayed capable battlefield management, he had been culpably negligent in the days leading up to the battle.

The soldiers directed considerable criticism toward the divisional commanders as well. As one Ohio soldier rightly wrote: 'the Generals...seemed to have no system', provided few orders and left the conduct of the fight in the hands of the field-grade officers. An Illinois soldier complained, 'There seems to be but little Generalship displayed, as the Enemy out-flanked us at the very onset.' In the absence of gener-alship, inexperienced regimental commanders had to confront the enemy to the best of their ability. Some, such as Thomas Ransom, Morgan Smith, Alvin Hovey, and Mortimer Leggett, showed a natural ability for combat and would rise far. Many others failed. Mistakes that could be laughed at on the drill field proved fatal in battle. The 15th Iowa was particularly dissatisfied with its field officer. 'The Col', recalls an Iowa soldier, 'does not know the difference between file right and file left and is as ignorant of Military Manoeuvres as a Child.' He added that the regiment's lieutenant-colonel drilled the regiment while 'under the inspiration of about a quart of old Commissary [whiskey]'. Incom-petence and drunkenness aside, the soldiers expected their officers to display courage at the very least. The battle exposed the cowards, and the soldiers hooted many of them out of the army.

The men who had fought at Shiloh began to think of themselves as veterans, and regiments that had performed well developed an *esprit de corps*. A soldier in the 32nd Illinois composed a poem in honour of his unit:

> *'It was on Shiloh's Bloody Field*
> *The 6th April Sixty Two*
> *The Rebels first Began to dread,*
> *The gallant Thirty two.'*

In a similar vein, an officer in the 2nd Texas Rifles proudly boasted that after his unit's gallant conduct, the regiment 'stands today ahead of all others in drill and discipline, and behind none in deeds of daring, valor and gallantry'.

Consequences for the South

In Richmond, from the time Johnston's army left Corinth until its return, no news arrived from Tennessee. Jefferson Davis considered this a very bad sign, believing that if his friend were alive he would have heard something. When confirmation of Johnston's death came, Davis broke down and wept. The nation had strained mightily to concentrate force in Tennessee and not only had that force failed, but the president's most trusted subordinate and admired friend had fallen, along with too many thousands of other dead and wounded young Confederate men. A gunner in Stanford's Mississippi Battery spoke for many when he wrote in his diary, 'What a pity that Gen. A. S. Johnston was killed. If he had not received that fatal wound, Grant and his army would have been

The absence of news from the west after 4 April persuaded President Jefferson Davis (above) that his good friend Sidney Johnston was in trouble. Later, Gen. Richard Taylor wrote of the impact of Johnston's death, observing that he was 'the foremost man of all the South' and that the cause was lost when he fell at Shiloh. (Tennessee State Library and Archives)

either killed, drowned in the Tennessee River, or taken prisoners'. Then and thereafter, Jefferson Davis shared this belief. With the clarity of hindsight, the president later observed, 'When Sidney Johnston fell, it was the turning point of our fate; for we had no other to take up his work in the West.'

Any replacement would have found it difficult to measure up to Johnston in the grief-stricken mind of the commander-in-chief. The detested Beauregard, who replaced Johnston, would have to provide near flawless performance to regain the president's trust. Instead, in the ensuing weeks Beauregard yielded western Tennessee. In fact, Halleck had concentrated an overwhelming force at Pittsburg Landing and then begun an exceedingly cautious advance against Corinth. His caution left little opportunity for anything but a Confederate retreat. However, to Davis, it seemed that 'Old Bory's' abandonment of Corinth undid the victory that was there for the grasping when Johnston fell. He concluded that the withdrawal was precipitous and the general unequal to the task at hand. When Beauregard left the army because of poor health, and did so without asking permission or notifying the commander-in-chief, Davis replaced him with Braxton Bragg. It was one of the few times he relieved a field commander, and it cemented the Creole's dislike for the president. Beauregard called Davis 'demented or a traitor', characterising him as 'that living specimen of gall & hatred.'

Braxton Bragg would lead the renamed Army of Tennessee for the next four major campaigns. He had absorbed certain lessons from Shiloh, the foremost of which was the need for discipline. His official report attributed defeat to a lack of 'proper organisation and discipline', and to a deficient officer corps. Unofficially, in a letter to his wife after

Halleck massed his forces to achieve a strength of 90,000 men and conducted a laborious advance on Corinth. (Library of Congress)

the battle, he reiterated the theme of poor discipline and inferior officers: 'Universal suffrage, furloughs & whiskey have ruined us.' Bragg's solution, stern discipline backed up by the firing squad, soon made him exceedingly unpopular among the rank and file. Worse, his inability to get along with his subordinates would consistently rob the army of the gains its sacrifices deserved. Henceforth, the Army of Tennessee – the guardians of the crucial Confederate heartland – would be the most ill-used of any major Civil War army.

From a southern perspective, Shiloh was a battle that had to be won. The Confederacy had stripped peripheral regions in order to concentrate at Corinth. In the words of Wiley Sword, 'The strategic objective had been to restore the lost balance of power in the West, to re-establish the Confederate frontier in Kentucky, and above all to save the vital Mississippi Valley.' None of this took place. Moreover, in the early afternoon of 6 April, the Army of the Mississippi had a real, but as the war would show, rare, chance to destroy an enemy field army. It was a devastating missed opportunity.

American Civil War battles in the west featured incredible carnage. Shiloh was merely the first in a series of memorable bloodlettings. Yet the majority of soldiers north and south would carry on. An Ohio soldier spoke for them in a post-battle letter to his father: 'I must confess that having one day's experience in dodging balls & shells & listening to the whistling bullets, I am not at all anxious to go into another fight. Still, if we do go into battle again you may rest assured I will do my duty faithfully.' North and South, soldiers and civilians who lived west of the Allegheny Mountains learned from Shiloh's carnage that war was cruel and that more of the same lay ahead.

Unable to check Halleck, Beauregard performed a skilful withdrawal from Corinth on the night of 29-30 May. He still had to burn or abandon large quantities of supplies. (National Archives)

THE BATTLEFIELD TODAY

Shiloh National Military Park offers the visitor an exceptionally rewarding historical experience. The park boundaries enclose 3,838 acres of the historic battlefield. Although time has eroded the 'sunken road', little else has changed since the battle. A 25-minute film at the visitor centre introduces the battle, and a driving tour from the centre highlights 15 stops. Taking the tour stops in order, however, puts the visitor out of the battle's chronological sequence. It is better to begin at Stop 7 in the Fraley Field, proceed to Stops 8 and 9, and then retrace the route to take in Stops 6, 4 and 3. Stop 3, Ruggles' Battery, has a superb collection of period artillery. Also take time to walk the lines of the Hornets' Nest before continuing to Stops 10-15, and finishing at Stop 1, Grant's Last Line.

As with any battlefield, nothing is better than to walk the ground. This writer, after a tiring day of hiking, found the dusk descent into Dill Branch a memorable reminder of the fatigue that afflicted Chalmers' men as they struggled up its steep slopes to engage the Federal gun line.

Shiloh National Military Park is located on State Route 22, 11 miles southwest of Savannah and 25 miles northeast of Corinth. Savannah, which retains the Cherry Mansion site of Grant's pre-battle head-quarters, offers satisfactory dining (catfish is a local delicacy) and overnight accommodation. A Civil War tour of central and western Tennessee can begin in Nashville, which is served by a major airport, and take in the Stone River Battlefield, Fort Donelson National Military Park, and Shiloh itself. From Shiloh, a more extended tour can drive down the historic Natchez Trace to Vicksburg and its splendidly preserved siege lines, or head east to Chickamauga and Chattanooga.

WARGAMING THE BATTLE OF SHILOH 1862

The main thing that makes this battle more than just another American Civil War scrap is the way both sides seem to have had very little overall control of the way it was fought. A combination of cluttered terrain, inexperienced troops, inadequate high level organisation and poor or inexperienced officers tended to lead to units doing pretty much their own thing.

The men themselves fought surprisingly well. Green Union troops attacked first thing in the morning when unprepared and with their flanks on air did well not running away. Hence there is no justification for downgrading troops even more.

The first thing to look at is the figures to use. There are a lot of very nice figures on the market at the moment. For this game I would go for one of the smaller scales, this allows larger units which spread more and cover more ground. This is an advantage in that it looks more reasonable when units break up in the difficult terrain. However, use the figures you have got. In 15mm there is a vast choice, in 6mm Irregular Miniatures and Heroics and Ross both produce excellent ranges which include virtually everything you can think of. Irregular Miniatures and especially Navwar also do ships for you to have in the river. If you are new to the period and are on a small budget Irregular Miniatures do a 2mm or 1/600 range. These are very small but en masse look effective and will get you cheaply into the period.

Once having chosen your figures, next build your terrain. Here you want something cluttered. There have to be enough open areas to provide fields of fire for defenders, but enough broken and difficult terrain to allow units to become strung out and make it difficult for officers to see what was happening. Normally one takes a level table and adds hills and clumps of trees to represent woods. Here I suggest you try something different. Take your table, put a few books or similar on it for the hills and undulations and then cover the lot with a green cloth. The green cloth can then represent scrub and broken ground. Scatter a bag of lichen over it to remind you. Then place some strips of a different colour cloth on top of the scrub. These are the clear patches. Effectively you are doing the exact opposite to what you normally do. Rather than assuming that everything is clear unless there is model terrain in place, you are assuming everything is scrub unless it is specifically marked as open.

Having got both figures and terrain the next thing to look at is the rules. There are many excellent sets on the market, as well as a lot of good 'house' rules about. So rather than tell you to try something different I will make a few suggestions as to how you can modify your current rules to give the proper feel of Shiloh. The aim is to enable you to get the feel of this particular battle, not merely fight another generic ACW bash over a historical terrain.

First let us look at the orders system. Armies break down into manoeuvre units. The size of these depends upon the period. In the First World War troops tended to be manoeuvred by brigade, in the Second World War by battalion. In Vietnam it was the company which was the self contained manoeuvre unit. At Shiloh for the Union forces it was the division which was the manoeuvre unit. Therefore you will write orders for the divisions. However, as Grant wasn't actually there, then there can be no orders written until he arrives at around the proper time. Up until then divisional commanders will act according to the dictates of their conscience. I would suggest that at some point in the game the divisional commander will be made aware that something is amiss. His outposts may have been driven in, or the sound of firing is heard by men in the division. He may even be warned by men from another unit streaming past in rout. At this point roll a six-sided die for the commander.

Union divisional commanders without orders table

Die Roll	Result
1	Commander panics and does nothing for two moves, roll again in two moves.
2,3	Commander stands his division to arms ready for orders.
4,5	Commander falls his men in defensive positions to protect his camp.
6,7,8	Commander marches his men to the sound of the guns.

You might wonder how you score 8 on a six-sided die. Basically allow the commanders of veteran divisions +2 on their die roll.

Another control issue is Buell's troops. Really you ought to have separate players for Buell and Grant. It would also help if they could only speak to each other when their figures were in base-to-base contact. As Buell's troops seem to have ignored those routing troops from Grant's army which fled back past them, then in the game routing Union troops only affect the army they belong to.

Confederate commanders had other problems. At least at the start of the battle they knew what their general wanted them to do. Not only that but they did have a corps structure, which means that the overall commander should have found the army easier to manoeuvre. This advantage was cancelled out by the way the army's overall command structure seems to have broken down once the fighting started and got tangled up in broken country. Each corps should therefore have written orders at the start of the battle. In 1st and 2nd Corps the divisions should have their own orders, effectively refinements of the corp's orders. In other corps there were no divisions so each brigade should have a copy of corps orders with occasional refinements.

When a brigade loses touch with the rest of its corps it must recheck its orders. 'Losing touch' I would define as getting more than an infantry move away from the rest of the corps and out of sight of it due to the terrain. Also if a brigade is obviously stuck with orders which are out of date and meaningless let it rest as well. Each brigade rolls a six-sided die.

Confederate brigade/divisional commanders table

Die Roll	Result
1,2	Halt in confusion and look for someone to tell them what to do next.
3,4	Continue to advance for two moves and then test again.
5,6	Advance to the sound of the guns.

Some of these results could do with a bit more definition. A brigade that halts in confusion will stop where it is and officers will scurry about looking for inspiration. Each move toss a coin. Heads they find a wandering staff officer who tells them to march to the sound of the guns. Tails, nothing happens, toss the coin again next move.

Marching to the sound of the guns is just that. The brigade/division will head as directly as possible to the nearest most impressive sounding battle. You have to use your judgement in this. A handful of troopers skirmishing with carbines may be nearer, but the infantry assaulting the Union batteries is far louder and more impressive. Hence they will advance to the sound of the more impressive batteries. It should also be noted that the sound of the guns they march to need not necessarily be the biggest threat to either them or the Confederate cause.

The only person who can override all this potential chaos is the Confederate commander. If he can ride up to a brigade, division or corps he can alter its orders and get it to do what he wants. All he has to do is get there in person or send a staff officer. This is where the terrain and clutter really comes into play. Remember right at the start of this section when discussing what figure scale to use I mentioned that we really wanted larger units which spread more and cover more ground. When the general or staff officer arrives at the erring brigade he still has to find the commander. If you represent your brigade by eight exquisite 25mm figures it looks a bit silly to say that the commander is difficult to find. If however the brigade is a straggle of 6mm figures half of which are lost in the lichen, then finding the brigadier is an obviously tougher proposition. Hence when the great man arrives at the brigade he leans down and asks the most presentable infantryman the whereabouts of the brigadier. Said infantryman pushes his hat back on his head and comments that 'half an hour back there was a horseman rode past them faster than spit off a griddle heading in that there direction'. This procedure continues until eventually the great man meets someone who saw the brigadier not two minutes ago. So when your staff officer or commander arrive at the brigade, toss a coin. On heads the commanders meet and can then start to exchange information and instructions. If you are trying to find a corps commander then roll a six-sided die and find the commander on a 5 or 6.

Another incident which had its effects on Confederate command and control was Johnston's death. I have played in games where the death of a general meant that the player commanding was immediately whisked away from the table while the rest struggled to work out who was in command. Most wargames rules cover this point well enough, and if you use the rules I have suggested above Johnston is going to spend an awful lot of time riding from one brigade to another and searching his front-line formations for their commanders. If the Union cannot kill him with all these opportunities then it is hardly my fault.

This nicely rounds up the chaos and confusion section. Now for some of the incidents. The first nice touch is the support fire of the US Navy Gunboats, *Lexington* and *Tyler*. These enfiladed the Confederate flank when the Confederates were pushing towards the Dill Branch and would certainly have been a serious presence if the fighting had got to Pittsburg Landing. Because of the size of the guns, their range, and the fact that navy pieces are often faster firing due to better facilities and larger crews, I would suggest treating each one as a 12-pdr. Napoleon battery at optimum range when firing at targets by the Dill Stream, and as Siege guns if the Confederates get to Pittsburgh Landing.

Another factor that has to be remembered is the Confederate troops propensity for breaking off to loot. Hungry and short of ammunition the Union camps they passed through were a great distraction. Hence I would suggest the following. Roll a six-sided die for each Confederate brigade as it passes through a Union camp.

Confederate actions			
Dice roll	In combat	Marching through	Halted
1,2	No effect	No Effect	10% drop out
3,4	No effect	10% drop out	30% drop out
5,6	5% drop out	30% drop out	50% drop out

Those figures that drop out are regained if the brigade halts for two moves outside the camp and waits for them to catch up. However, unless the brigade gets a halt-in-confusion result on the Confederate commander's table, or the commander in person intervenes, this isn't likely to happen.

So there you have it. I have tried to give you a few ideas which you can graft onto your favourite rules which make this battle of Shiloh. Hopefully for both sides but especially for the Confederates you will have great difficulty making your men do what you want. Perhaps when your men blunder about in the fog of war you will have a touch more sympathy for your predecessor who couldn't shelter behind the die, and had to intervene in person.

A GUIDE TO FURTHER READING

Daniel, Larry J., *Cannoneers in Gray,* Tuscaloosa, AL, 1984. The story of the Army of Tennessee's field artillery, with a fine chapter on Shiloh.

Esposito, Vincent (ed.), *The West Point Atlas of American Wars,* New York, 1959. Volume I includes the Civil War, with fine maps and good supporting text. Avery Publishing has an updated version in paperback.

Foote, Shelby, *The Civil War,* New York, 1958. Volume I of this well-written popular history devotes pages 314-351 to Shiloh.

Frank, J. and Reaves, G., *Seeing the Elephant: Raw Recruits at the Battle of Shiloh*, Westport, CT, 1989. A superb compilation and analysis of first-hand accounts.

McDonough, James Lee, *Shiloh: In Hell before Night*, Knoxville, TN, 1977. Decent general account, erroneous in some tactical detail.

Stillwell, Leander, *The Story of a Common Soldier of Army Life in the Civil War 1861-1865*, Erie, KS, 1920. Hard to find, but very worthwhile story of an Illinois soldier whose introduction to battle came at Shiloh.

Sword, Wiley, *Shiloh: Bloody April*, Dayton, OH, 1988. The best book-length treatment for tactical detail.

Throne, Mildred (ed.), *The Civil War Diary of Cyrus F. Boyd: Fifteenth Iowa Infantry,* Millwood, NY, 1977. Excellent account of the transition from civilian to soldier, with a good description of the panic of the first battle.

United States War Department, *War of the Rebellion: A Compilation of the Official Records of the Union and Confederate Armies,* Washington, 1884. Series I, Volume X, Part 1 contains the battle reports; Part 2 has the correspondence among the high command before and after the campaign. The 'ORs' are the indispensable starting source for any deep consideration of the war.

Watkins, Sam, *Co. Aytch,* New York, 1862. A Tennessee private's classic account. Watkins served in the 1st Tennessee from Shiloh until the end of Hood's ill-fated campaign in Tennessee, being one of seven (out of 120 soldiers in his company) to survive the entire war.

By their conspicuous presence and frequent displays of dashing courage, standard bearers made obvious targets for opposing marksmen. (National Archives)